Praise for *Chief Family Officer*

"*Chief Family Officer* stands out as a wonderful guide for entrepreneurial families who must strike a healthy balance between family dynamics and business ambitions. This book is a transformative journey into establishing connection-centric systems and structures within the home, fostering an environment where leadership and relational growth flourish side by side. Dave Inglis will help you step into the CFO role with confidence, skill, and compassion so you can create a thriving family unit that supports and enhances your family's cohesion, strength, and fulfillment."

JAYSON GADDIS, founder of The Relationship School and *Wall Street Journal*–bestselling author of *Getting to Zero*

"At the bedrock of your success sits your family. Dave Inglis teaches us how to not just bolster but bloom our most important relationships in *Chief Family Officer*, a must-read for every modern leader."

LAURA GASSNER OTTING, *Wall Street Journal*–bestselling author of *Wonderhell*

"Full of actionable advice, *Chief Family Officer* is a must-read for anyone trying to balance career and family. Dave Inglis connects with you on an emotional level while providing a practical approach to ensuring your family members get the attention they deserve."

MICHAEL STARK, founder of UnGrind

"As leaders, it is so easy to give much of our life force to our work and our mission that we often bring the scraps back home to our families. *Chief Family Officer* is not only a reminder to keep the main thing the main thing, but it also serves as a playbook for all of us to take what we know works in a business and apply it in the arena that matters most—our family life."

JAYSON GAIGNARD, cofounder and head curator at MasterMind Talks

"As a busy executive with a young family and a spouse who also has a growing business of her own, we live extremely demanding lives. Dave Inglis's *Chief Family Officer* provides invaluable insights on how we can buy back our time through a different mindset and build a family game plan. Truly relatable and very effective!"

TONY NGO, CEO of Collectivfide

"What's the value of a book? Well, in the case of *Chief Family Officer* by Dave Inglis, I'd say a better question is, What's the value of your life? Because, without a plan to manage your spouse, your kids, and yourself, you're on the fast track to losing it all. Make one of the best decisions you've ever made and use this book as your blueprint, before it's too late."

JAMES WHITTAKER, bestselling author, *Success* magazine speaker, and leading authority on how to Win the Day

"*Chief Family Officer* will give you the tools and the guts to build a family that is even greater than your business!"

RYAN BURGIO, managing partner at Stryve Digital Marketing

"Dave Inglis has written a must-read strategic plan for every high-performance leader that capitalizes on your leadership expertise to create the best family life you can imagine. Read the book and do the work—it is truly a game changer!"

KARA LIVY, president of Advanced Medical Solutions

"*Chief Family Officer* has been a game changer for our family. It focuses on nurturing your family's heart and soul amidst the hustle of daily life. Dave Inglis offers invaluable guidance on creating a harmonious family environment, where every member feels valued and connected."

DAWN L., CPA, CA

"Let's face it: we all want to be better for our families. We want to be better at showing up for our kids, and being present for our spouses. This brilliant book gives us the road map for how to actually *be* better. First by defining the problem, and then by giving a step-by-step action plan, Dave Inglis gives us the blueprint for taking our desire and making it a reality."

MIKE BROWN, founder of Unbreakable Wealth

"Your family is the foundation for success in all areas of life. Dave Inglis's honest storytelling allowed me to deeply connect with the content, and challenged me to think differently about how I lead my family and navigate the human condition."

ANDREW TURNER, Certified EOS Implementer at EOS Worldwide

"Dave Inglis's book triggers the personal aha! moment we all need to make a positive change in ourselves. *Chief Family Officer* uses relatable, personal, real-world storytelling to capture your attention and force you to challenge your own thinking. Anyone in a leadership position will gain many practical, applicable takeaways to implement in their own life. *Chief Family Officer* is a gold mine!"

DARRYL KING, president of JMP Solutions

"*Chief Family Officer* is an important guide that underscores the positive impact of prioritizing family leadership for success. Dave Inglis highlights how cultivating strong family connections is essential for a leader to not only support continued leadership development professionally, but also—and most importantly—personally at home. A recommended read for leaders who are seeking connection and relationship as leadership value."

MELANIE GUDMUNDSON, CHRO at Red River College

"Dave Inglis's *Chief Family Officer* isn't just a book; it's a road map to transforming our family lives with the same strategic brilliance we apply in the boardroom. Through practical wisdom and heartfelt stories, Inglis confronts the sobering reality that many executives awaken to only when it's too late—the realization that their families have drifted apart or are no longer there. He challenges us to prioritize what truly matters, inspiring us to become visionary leaders in our own homes. A must-read for anyone seeking to build a legacy of love and connection."

JEFF HORST, husband, father, and entrepreneur

"Do yourself a favor and put down that business book on business, and pick up this business book on family. *Chief Family Officer* is the reminder we all need... that family is #1."

ROB MACDONALD, entrepreneur and business broker

"Dave Inglis has packaged up his family leadership experience into a masterful playbook. His stories, frameworks, and next plays will help you run your home life with the same structure and fortitude that you bring to your work life. Chief Family Officer is probably the most important role we play."

CHRIS RONZIO, founder and CEO of Trainual

"*Chief Family Officer* is an insightful and practical guide that encourages families to create a shared vision, strategy, and system that promotes health and happiness. Dave Inglis provides approaches to help families create the environment for developing and sustaining structured practices, open communication, and alignment of individual and family values and goals."

JODI MEIERING, BBA, FCIP, CRM, COO
of Ayr Farmers Mutual Insurance Company

"I was excited to get my hands on Dave Inglis's book as I know how great he is at what he does. However, I was genuinely surprised at how frequently I had to stop reading and start talking to myself or my partner about a discovery that felt profound. This book is packed full of powerful ideas."

STEVEN FITZGERALD, president of Habanero Consulting Inc.

"*Chief Family Officer* will make you look at your family, business, and life priorities in a whole new way. Buckle up and enjoy the ride!"

MOATASSEM MOATEZ, founder and CEO of MYcourier

"Dave Inglis expertly demonstrates how the principles that guide successful businesses can be adapted to foster a thriving family environment. This book stands out as an essential resource for any business leader who recognizes that their paramount responsibility lies within the heart of their home. It's not just recommended reading—it's a vital playbook for excelling in the most crucial role of all."

MARK BLACK, CSP, coach, author, and speaker

"In *Chief Family Officer*, Dave Inglis takes us on a journey of self-discovery, vulnerability, and transformation. He shares real-life experiences, moments of triumph, and times of deep introspection where he confronts the turning points in his life, leaving an unforgettable mark and inspiring readers to embark on their own journey of self-discovery."

TODD MILLAR, president and CEO of TEC Canada

"Dave Inglis helps us rethink how we can invest in family, and encourages us to hone our craft as parents and spouses the same way we would as professionals running a thriving business. *Chief Family Officer* will help you set sail with a new game plan for running a healthy household and becoming the best version of yourself."

MICHAEL PERRY, founder and CEO of Maple

"Dave Inglis's *Chief Family Officer* has inspired me to become a better person and even importantly, a more supportive father. Through reading this book, I have made significant changes in how I approach family situations—and dramatically improved our family dynamic. I wholeheartedly recommend this book for anyone who wants to change their family dynamic in a realistic and transparent way."

JEFF BLANEY, COO of Waste Logic Inc.

"Winning in sport at the highest level requires a well-thought-out game plan. The stories and tools shared in this book will inspire you to extend a winning mentality to better lead your ultimate team—your family!"

MANDY BUJOLD, OLY, 2x Olympian and mom

"*Chief Family Officer* transforms the principles of corporate leadership into a profound strategy for crafting a fulfilling family life. Dave Inglis masterfully guides us through the journey of applying business acumen to the heart of home affairs, offering a fresh perspective on family dynamics. With compelling stories and actionable advice, Inglis challenges us to step into the role of Chief Family Officer with intention, leading to deeper connections, improved communication, and a family culture built on shared values and goals. This book is a must-read for anyone eager to bring their leadership skills home, creating a legacy of love, growth, and purpose."

MIKE DESJARDINS, CEO of ViRTUS Inc.

"This book is a breath of fresh air, loaded with real talk and practical advice, and it's got me thinking and acting in ways that are seriously leveling up our family life."

JOSIAH SHELLEY, entrepreneur and investor

"In *Chief Family Officer*, Dave Inglis has provided a fantastic framework for high performers to utilize in a way that enables us to shape the relationships that matter most in our families."

DUSTIN HEISE, CEO of Canada Snowboard

"*Chief Family Officer* gives you the tools through examples and thought-provoking questions to really look inside yourself to determine what winning looks like in order to have the beautiful life we are all searching for. Dave Inglis writes, 'The things you give attention and energy to will grow.' No truer words... after all, no matter how successful our business is, we are nothing without those we love to share it with—our family."

JOHANNA ALLEN, CAIB, CIP, president of Allen Insurance Group and CFO of Allen/Fraser Home

"Dave Inglis reminds us that winning at work doesn't mean winning at life. A call to action with a collection of captivating stories, practical examples, and a how-to road map to transform your home life and set you and your family up for success, happiness, and fulfillment."

GARTH CRESSMAN, P.Eng., MBA, CEO of WF Group

"I've read many business books but before reading *Chief Family Officer*, it never occurred to me to think about my family through a similar lens. The biggest aha! moment for me was the need to actively plan for family success versus just rolling with how life unfolds and hoping for the best. This book was a game changer for me. Dave Inglis is magic; he's impacted my life in so many positive ways. This book is a treasure."

LISA CASHMORE, partner and VP of ecosystem development at Regenerative Capital Group

"*Chief Family Officer* is more than just a book; it's a transformative guide that masterfully intertwines compelling storytelling with practical, hands-on strategies. This work stands out as a crucial companion for anyone aiming to cultivate a flourishing family life without sacrificing career success. It's a revolutionary read for those of us ready to assume the mantle of Chief Family Officer, converting everyday family challenges into opportunities for personal growth, deeper emotional connections, and authentic joy. An indispensable resource."

JESSICA WOODBECK, CEO of Thrive Realty Co.

"There is no team more important than your family. *Chief Family Officer* is a must-read strategic guide for leaders committed to putting their family first."

TRACY MACDONALD, president and CEO of Trillium Mutual Insurance

"We've run family meetings ever since our second son was born. They provide a beautiful opportunity to align on what's important, how we want to operate as a family (values, communication preferences, etc.), and table any important topics for discussion. What I love about Dave Inglis's approach in this book is how holistic and well-thought-out those meetings are. For families just starting out in this journey, and seasoned pros (like I'd like to believe my family is), this book is a gold mine of ways to level up."

CHRIS TAYLOR, president and CEO of Actionable

"*Chief Family Officer* is a comprehensive guide to leadership within the family unit. Through insightful anecdotes and practical advice, Dave Inglis emphasizes the significance of effective leadership skills grounded in empathy, communication, and collaboration. Inglis's approach highlights the transformative power of leadership rooted in love and understanding, making *Chief Family Officer* an invaluable resource for anyone seeking to put their family first in a world of conflicting goals and priorities."

MARK KULA, CPA, CA, VP of corporate development and strategy at Quadbridge Inc.

"This book is a wake-up call for business leaders who excel in their careers but struggle at home. Dave Inglis masterfully intertwines his authentic personal journey with transformative and actionable insights in a heartfelt invitation to redefine success, prioritizing our health and relationships as much as our careers. It's a moving reminder that our biggest achievements truly lie in the moments of effortless belonging we create with our loved ones."

KEVIN MAGEE, chief security officer at Microsoft Canada

"As someone who has personally implemented the strategies from *Chief Family Officer*, I can attest to its transformative power. This book is more than a guide—it's a journey that has profoundly impacted both my family life and my leadership at work. This book is now number one on my must-read list for all executives."

LUCAS ETHIER, EVP of PRIMED Medical Products Inc

"Take this book seriously, and your family will transform—starting with a more authentic, magnificent version of YOU."

MICHAEL CAZAYOUX, founder of Soul Searching Adventures

"This is your playbook to build a winning family team. With a mix of actionable tools and compelling stories, Dave Inglis gives a powerful invitation to step into your role as Chief Family Officer."

JESSICA CULLEN, managing partner of Regenerative Capital Group, professional triathlete, and Ironman Canada champion

"In *Chief Family Officer*, we are given the privilege of seeing, feeling, and knowing that this 'work of heart' is the greatest gift we can give ourselves and the ones that we love the most. In choosing to read this book, you are choosing to outlive, outshine, and out-love your former self!"

DR. JAMES ROUSE, speaker, author, coach, Emmy Award winner, and probably the happiest man on earth

CHIEF FAMILY OFFICER

Use Winning Plays from Work to Put Your Family First

DAVE INGLIS

CHIEF FAMILY OFFICER

PAGE TWO

Copyright © 2024 by Dave Inglis

All rights reserved. No part of this book may be reproduced, stored in a retrieval system or transmitted, in any form or by any means, without the prior written consent of the publisher, except in the case of brief quotations, embodied in reviews and articles.

Some names and identifying details have been changed to protect the privacy of individuals.

This book is not intended as a substitute for the medical advice of healthcare professionals. The reader should regularly consult a healthcare professional in matters relating to his/her/their health and particularly with respect to any symptoms that may require diagnosis or medical attention.

Cataloguing in publication information is available from Library and Archives Canada.
ISBN 978-1-77458-534-4 (paperback)
ISBN 978-1-77458-535-1 (ebook)

Page Two
pagetwo.com

Edited by James Harbeck
Copyedited by Jenny Govier
Cover design by Peter Cocking
Interior design by Cameron McKague

daveinglis.ca

First, I wrote this book for my future self. May I be a walking demonstration of my own advice and continue to find ways to become a stronger partner and parent.

To my wife, Jen, and my children, Quinn, Kalem, and William. There is nothing in the world I am prouder of than our relationship together. You inspire me to heal, grow, and bring my gifts to this world.

To all the people out there who are committed to a life of learning and growth. More than ever, our world needs leaders like you. Thank you for being willing to learn and do the work. It's never too late to begin again.

Contents

Foreword by Greg Wells, PhD *1*

1 Leading Your Most Important Team *3*

2 Your Family Will Change You *25*

3 It's Not What You Look at That Matters, It's What You See *47*

4 Playing to Win *69*

5 Using Pain as a Tool *93*

6 Protecting Your Most Important Asset: Relationships *115*

7 Designing Your Lived Experience *137*

8 Staying Connected and Aligned *161*

9 Beginning Again *183*

Acknowledgments *203*

Notes *207*

Foreword

WELCOME TO YOUR JOURNEY to becoming a Chief Family Officer!

In today's fast-paced world, it's easy to get caught up in the pursuit of success and forget about the importance of building a strong and loving family. But in this thought-provoking book, Dave Inglis reminds us that our family is our greatest treasure and that we have the power to create a beautiful family life by design.

I was in the room when Dave interacted with Philip McKernan at the Titan Summit—the experience he describes at the start of Chapter 2 of this book. I've been witness to Dave's evolution as a family man and business leader over the last few years. I am psyched to see that his growth has led to him writing this book and challenging all of us with the fundamental question: What is more important to us, building a big career or nurturing an incredible family?

With each chapter, Dave provides practical steps and thought-provoking questions that guide us in becoming the Chief Family Officers of our own lives. He encourages us to reconnect with our purpose, improve our leadership skills at home, and share inspiring stories that shape our identities as parents and leaders.

One of the key insights Dave shares is the importance of crafting a unifying vision for your family. By aligning your goals and aspirations, you create a strong foundation that motivates your family to change and grow together. He emphasizes the need to think about winning as a family in the present, near future, and long term, and he provides strategies for overcoming the challenges that may arise along the way.

I personally love Dave's idea of creating a Family Basecamp, where you and your family can discuss challenges and dreams while deliberately planning for the future.

He reminds us that success in implementing the lessons from this book is highly dependent on our spouse or partner being on board. By understanding their perspective and finding common ground, we can work together to build our family by design. My partner Judith and I have found this to be absolutely crucial to navigating our shared life.

I am honored to introduce you to this remarkable book, which has the power to change your perspective on family life and inspire you to take deliberate steps toward creating a beautiful and fulfilling family experience. Let Dave Inglis be your guide as you embrace your role as the Chief Family Officer and embark on a journey of love, growth, and connection.

Greg Wells, PhD
Author of *The Ripple Effect*; *Rest, Refocus, Recharge*; and *Powerhouse*
drgregwells.com

1

Leading Your Most Important Team

"**S**CREW YOU."

I punched the mailbox, mumbling the same words I had used to sign off the letter I'd just dropped in it. I wouldn't see or speak to my father again for nearly five years.

I grew up admiring my dad. I have vivid memories of being carried to the truck in the early weekend mornings to watch a race or go dirt biking together. Spinning on the big red chairs in the coffee shop, drinking hot chocolate and eating Timbits while my dad would get his early morning coffee and shoot the shit with the regulars. Waking up in the middle of the night running to my dad's truck in the rain to race to his shop when the security alarm would go off. When I was a kid, I had an insatiable hunger to hang out with my dad. But after my parents divorced in the late 1990s, we spent less and less time together.

As I grew into my teens, I was devoted to hockey. My dad, a second-generation business owner, was deeply devoted to his business. Over the years I would scan the stands from the ice, wondering if this would be the game my dad would finally come to. It never was.

During a playoff game, I landed on my head and fractured my C4 and T8 vertebrae. As I lay in the hospital bed strapped to a spinal board, my mom left the room to call my dad to share the news and ask if he could come see me. Unable to lift my head to see my mom when she returned to the room, I remember closing my eyes with tears pouring down my cheeks as she told me he wasn't coming to the hospital.

As I worked through my rehabilitation and gradually returned to day-to-day life, I saw my dad on the usual occasions and acted as if nothing was wrong. I had come to accept his absence as normal. But it ate at me.

When, a few years later, I wrecked my motorcycle—his motorcycle—trying to pop a wheelie, I lied and said I was the victim of a hit-and-run. I thought it might get me some sympathy. But as I sat in the back of my mother's van parked beside a Tim Hortons in Paris, Ontario, he came, picked up the motorcycle, put it in his truck, and left.

So I wrote him a letter. I punched the mailbox as I sent him my "screw you."

I was determined not to be like him. A seed was planted in me: a deep conviction to build a bigger and better business than my dad's and to become an incredible father myself. In my mind, self-achieved independence was the ultimate form of victory. That was now my new mission. Revenge is one hell of a potent motivator.

And I was mildly successful. While conducting concussion research for my undergraduate thesis in kinesiology, I quickly learned that I was atrocious at statistics and research but great at enrolling others in a vision and raising money. In my final semester of study, I partnered with my faculty supervisor to enter a pitch competition the business school was hosting, in pursuit of a small tranche of seed capital promised to the top three business ideas. I placed second and took home some cash and the confidence to continue exploring ways to commercialize our research. We created a business plan, pitched our idea for the Concussion Toolbox at pitch competitions across Canada, and ended up raising a meaningful amount of seed capital—enough to go all in on the business after I graduated and officially start my journey to becoming an entrepreneur.

As I entered my early twenties, I was building my venture and in a long-term relationship. If you had asked me then, I would have told you I was well on my way to winning and showing my dad that I didn't need his help to be successful.

And then I came home one evening in the early winter to find my girlfriend at the front door of our loft with several pieces of luggage packed. At first I thought she was surprising me with a vacation to get away somewhere warm together. But no. She was in tears, and her mother was in the parking lot. She was leaving me and moving back home.

While building the Concussion Toolbox, I had grossly overlooked my most important relationship. I was skipping date nights to work on proposals, answering emails during meals and movies, and working ridiculously long hours. She had had enough. The signs had been there all along, but, like a TV turned to the wrong channel, I wasn't seeing any of them. In my determination not to be like my father, I found myself behaving in a way I had sworn I never would. Now dealing with the consequences firsthand, I suddenly became aware of how complex the intersection of family and business was and recognized that I didn't understand my dad's full story. All I had were my own memories as a child—which, of course, lacked a tremendous amount of perspective.

The Intersection of Work and Home

Why did I decide to share this story with you? Because there is a 100 percent chance that every family will experience challenge, trauma, and change. My wife, Dr. Jen Forristal, teaches this principle well to parents in her book *The Umbrella Effect*: "There are many experiences in life that fall into the 'sucks but normal' category. Adversity, mistakes, imperfections, and hard feelings are normal and expected."

The reality is that my story is not unique. And yours likely isn't either. Although it was painful, the experience

I had with my dad falls into the "sucks but normal" category. And according to the United States National Center for Health Statistics, about half of all marriages will eventually end in divorce. The truth is, when it comes to long-term relationships, the odds aren't in our favor. Like bankruptcy, separation often happens gradually, and then quite suddenly. You have to actively create the environmental conditions that anticipate challenge and keep your family first, always. Families who don't do this will often find themselves disconnected for years, if not a lifetime. Now as I run two businesses, maintain a nurturing and highly secure relationship with my wife, and raise two teenage stepkids, a toddler, and a dog (fur babies count), I can tell you that just like a business, this doesn't happen by chance: the family you want is rarely what you get. You must actively work to build it.

Shortly after my girlfriend and I broke up, I headed on a solo trip to Hawaii to process how I'd ended up in this situation. After marinating in my own disappointment for five days, I found myself watching the sunrise on top of Haleakala, the 10,000-foot peak towering over Maui. It was in this moment that I knew I needed to do two important things after returning home to Canada.

First, I exited my business over the following year. I knew in my heart that I was in business for the wrong reasons and that it would never be successful if the motivation was coming from revenge and anger.

And second, I called my dad to apologize and ask for forgiveness. It had never been my intention to have my relationships or health become collateral damage in building my business. It happened quite gradually, and then quite suddenly. This experience opened my mind to the possibility that it wasn't my dad's intention either, and that it wasn't quite as simple as "Dad doesn't care about me or anything I'm interested in." My time away also made me appreciate how incredible a man my dad was and how hard he was working to provide for our family. I never told him I wanted more time together. If you don't ask, you don't get. It was pretty silly to expect him to be a mind reader. Not to mention that, as my dad went through divorce with my mom, I had never been there for him. I had never reached out to ask how he was doing. I began to see our common humanity, and I wanted to begin again.

After exiting my business, I was invited to teach entrepreneurship at Wilfrid Laurier University in Waterloo, Ontario, and I began consulting with corporate leaders to build their capabilities for corporate innovation and startup investing. It was often after a full day of strategy sessions and workshops with clients that I began to connect personally with the corporate leaders over a glass of wine and a bite to eat.

When asked how I came to do the work I was doing, I would openly share the personal journey I had gone through. Often surprised by my vulnerability and openness, leaders would lean in and share the personal challenges they were facing at home. As I learned about their stories, I would acknowledge the great work they put into their business and then ask, "When was the last time you invested this amount of time and energy into your most important team: your family?" Throughout your career, you will be a part of, and lead, many different teams. Some for a short while, and others for many years. But your family—you have a seat on that team for your entire life. Your family is the team that is there for you when you win big or lose it all and when you are in the corner questioning who you are and what you should do next. There is no team that could ever be more important.

Over the next three years, I continued to have conversations like that as I met and worked with some of the smartest people in the world—people leading military organizations such as the Royal Canadian Air Force; publicly traded corporations such as TD Bank, GM, and Fairfax; and some of the fastest-growing startups—and I started to observe a pattern.

When it came to leading their teams at work, most of the leaders I worked with were real pros. Need to turn around a failing business strategy and guide a few hundred people through change? No problem. Have hard conversations with clients and key team members to right a wrong, get aligned, and move forward? Piece of cake. Delegate key jobs that will create more capacity to work on projects with more ROI? With pleasure.

Yet when it came to their most important team, their family, they were quietly struggling. Even worse, their struggle at home was subtly sabotaging their ability to bring their best to their vocation. Susan, a CFO from a global consumer packaged goods company I worked with, shared a story with me that illustrates this beautifully:

Back in 2019, our CEO was let go suddenly after failing to hit our quarterly targets four quarters in a row. As the CFO, I was asked to step in to lead the organization as interim CEO for about six months while the board recruited a new leader to turn around the company. A few weeks in, I was greeting several directors who were arriving for a quarterly board meeting I was hosting and remember looking down at my Apple Watch to see a text message from my husband that read, "WTF?" accompanied by a photo of my daughter's empty lunch bag. While racing to get to the office early that morning, I had forgotten to make my daughter's lunch. Already anxious for my board meeting, I felt my stomach sink. My husband was pissed. After asking our board to delay our meeting by five minutes, I stepped out to call my husband to get things sorted. I remember hanging up the phone and returning to the room feeling overwhelmed and distracted. After I'd prepared for the last week, the phone call with my husband totally threw me off my game. And I knew this would continue to drag out that night when I got home, as usual. How the hell can forgetting to make a sandwich get in the way of making multi-million-dollar decisions at work?

One of my dear friends, Phil Jones, always says, "When you are impressed by someone, don't say *wow*, ask *how*." And that's exactly what I started to do. Regardless of the industry, leaders who were winning in business demonstrated many of the same qualities. They had a growth mindset and actively sought out opportunities to put themselves in a position to be challenged. They intentionally surrounded themselves with a community of peers to learn from. They were continuously reading new books and enrolling in programs to advance their skills. They considered winning a team sport and hired expert coaches and consultants to help them navigate difficult decisions. They possessed the intellectual humility to honestly evaluate their behaviors and uncover opportunities to get better. They weren't victims of circumstance, but instead took absolute personal responsibility and were the authors of their own stories. And most importantly, they had a clear definition of what it meant to win. Yet when I asked how they were approaching their family life, it was as if I were speaking to an entirely different person.

I had always thought that how you do one thing is how you do everything. I was learning that this just isn't true. Most leaders are extremely ambitious and deeply committed to changing the world for the better, but they are failing to bring their leadership home. As someone who had experienced this firsthand, I could see the hypocrisy of the ambition to be a great business leader when I was failing where it mattered the most. There isn't a team or organization more deserving of your leadership than yourself and your family. Your family is the most important team in the world. When you get this right, it creates the foundation to build your dreams from. You need to bring the same C-suite focus and dedication to your family. You need to become a Chief Family Officer.

In my experience, I've never met a leader who intentionally neglects their family. So, how does it happen? Why is it so difficult for leaders to bring their incredible leadership skills home with them from work?

Core Challenges

When it comes to managing a business, we know there are a handful of core challenges a leader must overcome to build a scalable, repeatable, and profitable business. Gino Wickman, author of *Traction* and founder of the Entrepreneurial Operating System, describes the five key challenges as lack of control, misaligned team members, insufficient profits, stagnation, and wrong strategy or tactics. Similarly, leading a family comes with five key challenges, although they are very different.

My mother-in-law, Brenda, often says, "If people knew better, they would do better." And I believe it! No one gets into business actively seeking the empty victory of becoming an unfulfilled high performer. But if we aren't aware of the obstacles getting in the way, it is difficult to make better choices. And when we make better choices, our results and lived experience change. When you make the choice to take on the role of Chief Family Officer and lead your family, there are five core challenges you must be prepared to overcome.

1 No Shared Vision of What It Means to Win

Any leader worth their weight will tell you how important it is to build and communicate a clear and strong vision. Without a clear definition of what it means to win as an organization, teams become misaligned and begin to work against each other, lose focus, and drift off course.

Strategy creates the container and clarity for a business to thrive. As Roger Martin, author of *Playing to Win*, says, every strategy has to begin by answering one simple question: "What is your winning aspiration? What does it mean to win?" To design and build anything great, you must always start with a clear definition of success. Without it, it's almost impossible to define your priorities and confidently make good decisions. So, when you imagine your family at its best, what do you see?

When it comes to family, most leaders have a great understanding of what it means for *them* to win personally, but they have never had a conversation with their spouse and kids to define what it means to win *together*, as a family. In the absence of a clear definition of what it means to win, it is easy for your family members' dreams and aspirations to lay dormant and, without ill intent, become secondary to your own personal aspirations. Having now coached hundreds of leaders, I can tell you most of the day-to-day conflicts between spouses are easily solved by building a compelling and shared vision for the future together. You can work on communication skills all you want, but if you don't have a clear destination and family lens to lead from, you will always be arguing about what turn to take next: "me versus you" instead of "us versus it."

In this book, I will challenge you to co-create a family strategy with your spouse. The clarity that comes from defining your family's winning aspiration, core values, and three-year picture will create the context for every other decision you make as a family. It will position your family to work together to overcome challenges. When you get this right, it changes everything.

2 Lack of Accountability

In business, accountability is built into every system and process, so it affects how you show up and the decisions you make. Whether it's the CEO, a VP, or the board of directors, you have a leader to report to. There is oversight and continual awareness that the results of your behaviors will be judged and evaluated by others. If you fail to respectfully engage your clients and team members, they'll leave you to work with someone else. When the stakes are high like this, most leaders enter what Jayson Gaddis, executive coach and founder of the Relationship School, calls "strategic self" and practice high levels of self-regulation and executive function to maintain strong relationships in a way that gets rewarded and praised. Like in a group workout, we up our game when others are watching.

However, when it comes to your family, there is significantly less accountability and fewer rewards for strong leadership. There is no annual review to discuss what you're doing well and where you could improve. And there aren't many carrots or sticks. No bonus is awarded to you for retaining your spouse for another year. At work we thoughtfully navigate conflict because we know customers or employees can leave us at any time, and the cost of that to us is significant. When it comes to family, we tend to do the opposite: we assume our family will never leave us because "we're family." We take this for granted. It's incredible how patient and understanding we can be with a customer and impatient or reactive moments later with the people who really love us.

To overcome this challenge, you must create your own accountability. Unlike in other environments, where you can rely on external sources of accountability, to be the leader your family needs you must set your own standards and practice self-leadership to hold yourself accountable. I will show you how to regularly evaluate your leadership and the well-being of your family to make sure you continue to adapt and move toward your winning aspiration. The good news? You'll become a better business leader along the way.

3 Not Enough Time in the Day

In a high-performing team environment, every team member has a clear area of responsibility and the opportunity to focus on performing exceptionally well in one key area. As the demands on your team grow, it is easy and common sense to invest capital to expand your team capacity and take on more. Depending on the project, you can bring on contractors to get things done, acquire another business, or scale up a new division or team.

Most families are off track and overwhelmed at the best of times. Ask any parent, and they'll say there is never enough time in a day. Parents are often left making decisions between spending quality time with their kids, folding laundry, taking the dog for a walk, answering emails, racing to and from sports, and making a quick run to the grocery store. Layer in a sick child or an impending work deadline, and you're toast. I often say, "You can do anything, but not everything." And even if leaders have a high enough annual income to afford extra help (nannies, landscapers, cleaners), many struggle to overcome the emotional obstacle of feeling deserving of this help—or more often a sense of guilt for not taking on everything themselves, like their parents and grandparents did.

The traditional family model of one working parent and one at home is no longer commonplace. While total family income is on the rise, the capacity to take care of and manage the day-to-day of a family is shrinking. Our culture is evolving, but there is a good chance your family's systems are far behind. To overcome this challenge as a leader, it is critical that you learn how to create more capacity for your family. I wrote this book to show you how.

4 Failing to Repair after Conflict

I mentioned earlier the idea of a strategic self. Like turning on a "presentation mode," the strategic self is akin to putting on a mask to strategically bring forth a set of qualities or attributes to navigate a particular situation or circumstance. In business, this is common. Whether it's a meeting with your boss, a presentation you are giving to a client, or a collaboration with another department, "getting the job done" is far more important than "getting along" or connecting at a deep personal level. Our relationships and connections are often secondary to achieving an outcome. Because of this, we act like chameleons, ever changing ourselves to achieve the goal.

However, when it comes to building a strong, secure, and loving family, the primary goal *is* connection. Unlike most professional relationships at work, our relationships at home are attachment based, which means you are each other's secure base and safe haven. It is in these relationships that our early attachment patterns of security or insecurity surface very naturally. Your spouse will bring out the darkest parts of you—parts that you might not have known exist. More than your parents. More than your best friend. More than your kids. And more than your team at work. During a recent couples experience my wife Jen and I hosted, Jayson Gaddis captured it well when he said, "The person sitting beside you right now [your partner] is your soul mirror and a total pain in the ass at times. And should you choose, they will become a beautiful teacher who will help you become a more authentic version of you."

Most people have been misled to believe that conflict is a bad thing, a sign of things falling apart and an unhealthy relationship. Even worse, we've been taught that once we fall in love, all the hard work is done and we can now ride off into the sunset of happily ever after. Wrong. Building a strong and successful family is much like owning a house. There is some upfront work to get things built, but your most important relationships require ongoing maintenance if you want to successfully navigate and grow from the challenges you will face. And you must understand that conflict is the only way to build a strong and secure family. To navigate conflict well, you must master the art of conflict repair.

Throughout this book, I will challenge you to uncover the life experiences that have informed the way you disconnect when conflict shows up. Once you've done this, you'll need to learn how to lead your family through conflict by standing up for yourself, those you love, and your collective family unit—what Jayson Gaddis calls "Standing for Three." After reading this book, you will see conflict as a key ingredient in strong relationships—and become a student of conflict yourself.

5 Waiting on Your Partner to Change

The culture of our families today has significantly changed from the traditional breadwinner/homemaker dynamic of the 1950s. According to Stats Canada, in 2014, 69 percent of couple families in Canada with at least one child under sixteen were dual-earner families. This was up from 36 percent in 1976. Today, couples are challenged more than ever to collaborate to get everything done. Yet while much has changed, a "she-fault" dilemma is still very much at play: more women are working, yet a disproportionate amount of family responsibility still defaults to the woman in a heterosexual couple. While this may not perfectly illustrate the dynamics of your home, the important point to reflect on is that in relationships, the responsibility to take care of your house and family is often skewed to one individual more than another. Over time couples begin to take note and keep score of all the things their partner does or doesn't do. Unless there are clear agreements in place, a large gap here makes leading together difficult.

When it comes to leading and building your family together, you and your partner are a system, not an individual. This means that the two of you will inherently have different viewpoints, beliefs, and approaches about the right way of doing things. In the absence of a practice that unifies this system together, most leaders blame their partner for the lack of harmony or joy in their home. "If only she would be more present around the house. Until that gets resolved, why would we even bother to talk about our vision for the future?" Or, "If he would start helping around the house a bit more, everything would be easier." Many couples haven't started to work on their family because they are waiting for their partner to change.

If you want to build a family you are proud of—a family you absolutely adore—instead of waiting for them to change, you must instead allow your spouse or kids to change in the process of this work. Playing the waiting game is a disempowering position to be in. To lead means you must take the first step. When you take the first step and begin to actively work on your family, the work will naturally create opportunities to inspire your family members to grow individually and collectively along the way. Remember, the work works on you more than you work on it.

Your Family Operating System

A key tool in your success as Chief Family Officer is a well-running family operating system: a complete set of tools and proven processes to empower you and your spouse to build your family by design—a practice to overcome adversity, adapt to new and changing circumstances, and intentionally grow your wealth, health, and relationships along your journey.

In a computer, an operating system is a program that manages all the other application programs. It is responsible for managing the computer hardware and software resources, and it provides common services for computer programs to run effectively day to day. Today, we take for granted the complex operating systems that power our laptops, cell phones, and various technology platforms like the dashboards in our cars. But the earliest electronic systems had no operating systems at all until the early 1960s. This meant that a computer could only operate one program at a time, unlike the dozens of applications that our iPhones use at any one time. As the demands on computers became more complex, operating systems played a critical role in expanding the technology's ability to do more at one time. A well-functioning operating system is invisible but keeps everything running smoothly.

But operating systems don't just show up in our cell phones and computers. A great example of this is EOS, the Entrepreneurial Operating System. EOS was created by Gino Wickman to help entrepreneurs get control of their businesses. When you start a business, there is a point where you hit a ceiling, and the business owner becomes a bottleneck. As you bring on more customers, grow your revenue, and expand your team, you can no longer thrive by winging it day to day or leaving every decision up to a single leader. At some point, your velocity as a company begins to slow down, and the risk for poor decision making increases exponentially. Successful entrepreneurs understand that to overcome this, they must install a business operating system: a structured way of defining priorities and goals, adapting to new information or challenges, allocating resources, and making important decisions. EOS is a complete set of simple concepts and practical tools that help entrepreneurs do just that, and get more of what *they* want from their business. It is a proven system used to get everyone in the business on the same page and stay focused on what's important to execute, while managing the health and cohesiveness of the leadership team. It isn't a computer operating system; it's a *people operating system*. When you choose to adopt an operating system for your business, it empowers you to build the business by design and make sure everyone is working toward the same goal.

It's the same when it comes to your family. When it's just you and your spouse, it's pretty easy to collaborate day by day. You can adjust in the moment and connect on an as-needed basis. But, as with a computer or business, as the load gets bigger, you need an operating system to manage your capacity and make sure the right things are getting done.

When you embrace your role as Chief Family Officer, the family operating system I am giving you in this book will help you to lead your family in three important areas:

1. **Family strategy:** This is where you will learn how to create the clarity your family needs to make important decisions, such as where to live, how you earn an income, who to spend your time with, and how

you will win as individuals and as a family. When your family understands what it means to win together, you create the context for everything.

2. **Systems of living:** A strategy and vision without a clear execution plan is delusional optimism. You will develop systems of living: things you do day to day and week to week to make everything work, keep everyone aligned and supported, solve emerging issues, and buy back your time to do more of what you love.

3. **Relational excellence:** Conversations and conflict are the only pathway to building strong, secure families. You will learn how to proactively invest in your most important relationships, use pain as a tool, and create a culture that empowers your family to have the conversations so many avoid.

Two Pathways Forward

I have coached and worked with thousands of leaders around the world over the last decade. These experiences have taught me that you have two pathways forward when it comes to becoming a better leader. And you need to make a choice.

The first pathway is to focus your development efforts on becoming a stronger leader at work. For most people, this path is filled with new challenges and exciting opportunities that lead to promotions, industry recognition, and big raises. But the brutal reality is that most of this success often comes at the cost of your health and relationships. And seldom, if ever, does your leadership development translate into you becoming a better partner, parent, or friend. If you are on this path right now, it probably feels like your career is dragging your life and family like a tube behind a boat. Sounds fun at the beginning, but it gets old pretty quick. Especially if the waters are choppy.

The second pathway is to make the choice to become a great Chief Family Officer and improve your leadership skills to better lead your most important team: your family. Our world doesn't need more business leaders right now, but it desperately needs stronger community leaders, which starts at home. And the good news? If you make a choice to become a great Chief Family Officer, not only will you create a foundation and competitive advantage for your family members to launch off of, but your own personal growth and leadership development will translate back into your business and help you win there too.

So let me simplify your choice. What is more important to you: building a big business or an incredible family?

If your main focus is building a big career, go for it. I wish you well, send you my biggest love, and suggest that you give this book to someone you care for, because the remaining chapters won't be much use to you. There are plenty of other books out there that will show you how to work on personal branding or build a new product offering.

But if you're ready to start leading your family, building your family by design, and playing to win at home, you're in the right place.

Next Play

At the end of each chapter, I am going to share with you the Next Play: a series of questions and activities designed to help you apply this work in your own life. Growth doesn't happen by chance. You need to make this work your own, so to get the most out of this book, have a dedicated journal or Word document where you can engage with the questions and exercises I am going to provide along the way.

The first play is to reconnect with why you're here.

1. Why did you pick up this book? Why now?

2. How will improving your leadership at home help you win at work?

3. What is a story you can share that explains what inspires you to become the parent and leader you want to become?

2

Your Family Will Change You

"WHO IN THE ROOM has been struggling to make a change?" he asked.

My hand shot up like someone else had raised it for me.

Every year I challenge myself to attend at least one leadership conference to expand my community and learn from some of the greats. At this moment I was at Robin Sharma's Titan Summit in Toronto, and one of the keynote speakers, Philip McKernan, was breaking into his Q&A after talking about "soulset" (the connection you have to something bigger than yourself) for the last ninety minutes.

At the time, I was struggling to decide whether to start my own coaching practice after consulting and teaching entrepreneurship at Wilfrid Laurier University.

It had been five years since my trip to Hawaii. Standing in front of about a hundred entrepreneurs and leaders in the middle of the Ritz-Carlton ballroom, I reluctantly shared my situation.

"Okay, Dave. I'd like you to think about someone really important in your life."

I looked up at Philip and nodded.

"Who is it?" he asked.

While exiting my business and navigating a big career change, I had met, fallen in love with, and married Jen. As if trying to figure out my professional life wasn't enough, I had unexpectedly found myself taking on a new role as an "insta-dad" to two incredible kids, Quinn and Kalem. With my heart beating in my throat, I grabbed the microphone and said, "My stepdaughter Quinn. She's an incredible kid, nine years old and heading into grade five next year."

"Wonderful. So I'm wondering... how painful is it for you to be a corporate innovation consultant? On a scale of 1 to 10, give us a sense of how you would rate your day-to-day experience."

Skeptical that this was a trick question, I took a moment to collect my thoughts. While it wasn't *exactly* what I wanted to be doing, my job wasn't that bad. In fact, it was pretty good. I was making great money and working on exciting projects with people I respected, and I had a once-in-a-lifetime opportunity to build one of the world's largest corporate innovation centers. For the most part I had great control of my time, and I had the flexibility to work remotely, making it easy to travel and do the things I loved. I held up three fingers and looked around the room. All eyes were on me.

"Brilliant. It sounds like you've got a pretty good gig right now. So, let's fast-forward for a moment. Just imagine we are ten years in the future and Quinn is now nineteen years old, starting her second year studying at university. She comes home at Thanksgiving, and after dinner one night she opens up to you and shares that she really doesn't like the field of study she selected. She is starting to consider switching into an arts degree to follow her love of writing and fine arts. Much like you, she is quite successful in her studies right now, but it doesn't light her up. What would you say?"

I knew exactly how I would handle the situation. With conviction I quickly responded, "Well, in my opinion, you always finish what you start. So I would tell her that she should finish out this semester but schedule an appointment with her academic advisor right away to begin the process of switching degrees. There is no sense in dragging out a degree to start a career she doesn't love. Discovering what you want to do is part of the university experience. If she is doing something that she truly loves, she can't fail!"

The room fell quiet as we waited to see where Philip would go from there. "Well, Dave, I think you have two options. You can wait ten years to have that conversation with Quinn, or you can lead by example right now so you never have to. Or, more likely, you can have that conversation without Quinn rolling her eyes and mumbling, 'Oh yeah Dave, because you're such a great example of following your dreams.'"

As tears fell down my cheeks, the pain of staying in my job suddenly went from a three to a ten. For about a year I had contemplated this change in private. As much as I knew I wanted to make the change, when I'd explored the possibility through the lens of how it would serve me, I'd always seemed to have a good reason to justify why it wasn't the right time. And even on the days I could acknowledge there never would be a perfect time, I'd found another reason why I was unqualified to make the jump, or better yet, I'd get fixated on how unfair and selfish it was for me to expose my new family to the financial risk of starting a new business. It was like putting a kernel of popcorn over a hot stove but pulling it away as soon as it got hot. Until this moment. When I shifted my focus to someone I loved, my kernel popped.

When I returned to work five days later, I sat my team down and shared my decision to start my own coaching business, and I gave them a six-month transition notice. I didn't know *exactly* how I was going to do it, but I knew that if I made the choice and gave myself a runway, I would figure out how to grow into the person I wanted to become.

Having a family will change you. It can be the reason you avoid your dreams, or it can be the reason you pursue them and put everything on the line.

Who Do You Want to Become?

Do you know what you want in life? I believe most people know exactly what they want. More of this. Less of that.

And many even have detailed plans about how they could make it happen. Yet, they don't act. Months and years go by as their dreams remain idle, waiting for the perfect moment when everything lines up.

When it comes to turning into the person you want to become, the real challenge is learning how to overcome the unseen obstacle of fear that comes from abandoning certainty. Whether it's deciding to get sober, starting your own business, separating from your spouse, or moving to a new city, the fear of the unknown will rear its ugly head. Expect it. If you're the type of person who is committed to growth, you must learn how to navigate and overcome this inner tension. And here's the big idea. Just as Philip did for me, you must make the reason to change about someone else. Because if it's for you, you likely won't have a big enough reason and purpose to match or overcome your internal resistance and anxiety for real change. As podcaster Chris Williamson said, "Give a man a purpose and the ability to achieve it, and he will crawl over broken glass with a smile on his face."

Vanilla ice cream tastes great with pie, but it shouldn't be how you describe the life you build for yourself. This is why I am so committed to my own personal development. I want my kids to embrace their unique gifts and talents and do the work to design their own lives. And the best way to do that is to become a living demonstration of the courage that is required to step away from "good enough." Throughout this book you are going to acquire plenty of tools, big ideas, and frameworks to put your family first, but you need to come to this work with motivation and a "why." Without a clear reason, your kernel will never turn into popcorn. And if you ask me, unpopped kernels taste like shit.

Over time, you are going to have to adapt how your family operates to stay attuned to and aligned with the priorities and needs of those you love—including your own. There are different seasons to life, and in each of them your context and circumstances will change. This means that the type of support your family needs today might not make sense next year. The amount of space you have to invest in your marriage will expand and contract as your personal and professional commitments come and go. Instead of looking for the "right answer," we want to ask, What is the right answer *now*?

Most people make the mistake of working on their family to solve problems that are making life difficult and getting in the way of their career. The goals we typically set are negative in nature. "I want my husband to stop yelling at our kids," or "I want to feel less guilty for taking time away from my family." When our motivation to change something is to eliminate a problem, we seldom see long-term change. Let me explain.

Let's imagine you have the goal to lose some weight. You pulled out your clothes for the upcoming winter, and when you tried on your favorite pair of jeans, things were a little tight. As you look at yourself in the mirror with frustration, you make the commitment to lose weight so you can feel good again in the clothes you love. After hiring a trainer and cleaning up your diet for three months, you successfully lose ten pounds and your pants feel great again. At first you are elated, but about six months later you've added on the weight again, and just as spring rolls around, you are back to square one.

As soon as the source of shame and frustration is gone (because of our hard work), the original source of motivation is no longer there to continue fueling our long-term behavioral change. When we commit to change to get away from a negative feeling, the fuel source for our motivation is like race fuel. It will blast us off the starting line, but it will lack sustainability to go the distance. It doesn't matter if it's finances, weight loss, or anger management—this is why so many people oscillate between making progress and regressing to old norms.

If you want to make sustainable behavior change, you must set a much bigger vision and positive goals, where "losing weight" is simply a part of the process. So how do you do this?

By asking one simple question: "Who do I want to become?"

When we set a positive goal that clearly illustrates who we want to become, our fuel source and motivation to do the work shifts, and we start to build a sustainable long-term relationship with our commitment. Instead of setting a goal to get out of debt, we can craft a positive vision statement, such as the following:

I am becoming someone who can focus at work all day, always has the energy to play with my kids, can manage my emotions during conflict, and has the ability to embark on adventures to explore the world through sport.

or

> *I am becoming someone who is increasing her net worth each and every day, has the health and vitality to live for more than a hundred years, and has secure and strong relationships with her friends and family.*

This is really important to understand, because this book is going to have a profound and positive impact on you and your family. When it does, I don't want your motivation to continue working on your family to go out the window.

Here is a visual to help you see the two different ways of approaching this work. One lens is to view this work as a series of linear problems to solve. Much like in a Spartan race, you can view building your family as an obstacle to overcome in pursuit of a finish line. The challenge with this is that we believe that once it's done, we can move on and never think about it again. Instead of visualizing yourself overcoming a series of obstacles, I would encourage you to use the other lens: imagine you are climbing a spiral staircase. The problems you are going to solve together are cyclical in nature. While you will continue to grow and ascend every step you take, you can expect that life will challenge you to revisit these obstacles more than once.

The person who loves walking will always walk farther than the person who loves the destination. The work works on you more than you work on it. When we think of this work as a project, it is easy to become frustrated when we have to revisit a subject we thought was behind us. The spiral staircase image helps us expect challenges and stay focused on the journey and who we are becoming.

When you get this right, it positions you to become an anti-fragile family—a family that benefits from challenge and increases its capability to thrive as a result of the inevitable stressors, mistakes, faults, and volatility inherent in the human experience. Building your family is a journey that happens day by day, moment by moment. Every day you have the opportunity to begin again. And for better or for worse, this journey will change you. Choosing to lead your family will be the greatest catalyst for your personal development.

Coming Home

Growing up, I loved playing hockey. But I loved singing and playing music even more. From my earliest memories, I sang in the school choir and played the saxophone and drums in our school band. Practicing scores of music over and over came easy to me. I loved the pressure of performing in front of large audiences. And then, in grade eleven, I suddenly decided to quit.

I remember telling my teacher, Ms. Kathy McNaughton, that I was tired and wanted a break. The real reason? I had recently got a new girlfriend who was a year older than me. I wanted to fit in with her friend group and, well, let's just say that singing in the school choir and playing in the band wasn't cutting it.

Whether it's with our parents, our friends, or our colleagues, all of us have an innate desire to experience *effortless belonging*. I personally think of effortless belonging as being able to let your hair down and feel safe to express your true self without fear of abandonment or judgment. But I had to learn this the hard way. As Brené Brown eloquently points out, "Fitting in is about assessing a situation and becoming who you need to be to be accepted. Belonging, on the other hand, doesn't require us to change who we are; it requires us to be who we are." While the circumstances are always different, we all learn at some point to fit in by modifying our self-expression and becoming a strategic version of ourselves. After ditching my love of music, the real friendships I had made over many years began to gradually wither away. Shortly after my girlfriend moved away for university, I learned that she was cheating on me with a guy she had met in her dorm. Now alone and heartbroken, I realized how much I had given up to fit in. It wasn't worth it. And it never is.

One of my personal mentors, Jayson Gaddis, describes your strategic self as a "modified self-expression" you can turn on to blend in and reduce the risk of being disconnected or experiencing conflict. While in the short term this creates positive feedback from your peer group, over time an inner conflict emerges as you start to experience anxiety and depression from constantly trying to be someone you aren't. And unfortunately, this compounds over time once you enter the workforce and begin fighting for promotions and new opportunities to succeed. As the carrot gets bigger, you become hyper-sensitive to the reactions from your bosses, clients, and team members to gauge what resonates and what doesn't.

Don't get me wrong; sometimes you just need to turn it on. The issue is that, over time, most people fail to turn off their strategic self and gradually lose the ability to share their true self-expression. As with a muscle that atrophies over time from not being used, they forget who they truly are. When your strategic self is who comes home to your family every day, it's nearly impossible to create an environment of effortless belonging. In business, winning is measured by achievement. But when it comes to your family, winning is all about creating moments and experiences of effortless belonging—for yourself and for the people you love most.

Take a moment to digest the reflections from one of my clients, Andrew, after he became VP of a fast-growing startup. On the outside, Andrew has everything he ever wanted: A family. Lots of money in the bank. A beautiful house. A few vacations every year. But notice the inner conflict he is experiencing:

I was really excited when I accepted this job as VP a couple years ago, but I don't think I want to run this division anymore. We've got two kids right now, eleven and six. Our youngest son has been a lot for our family to manage over the last few months, and it's been wearing us all down. He's been struggling with his temper, and I want to give him more of my presence and emotional support—but I just can't seem to do it. My wife, Alyssa, always gets so frustrated with me when I'm on my phone around the kids, but I have to always be available to my team. If I'm not able to answer questions right away, I hold them back from getting things done, or worst case they will go ahead without my feedback and screw things up. Even when I'm alone, I seem to always be picking up my phone to flip through the news. I feel like I can't win. I am either with my family and letting down my team, or I'm with my team and letting my family down.

You can feel his frustration, can't you? Most of my clients are very quick to look for solutions and fixes. But when we are moving through challenges in life, it is important that we seize the opportunity to learn more about ourselves in the process. So when you are working to change something, take the time to also reflect on: "How is the current way I've been doing this serving me? And where did I learn it from?"

Andrew's response illustrates how our strategic self helps us manage our anxiety and worry, but at the cost of our well-being and integrity:

How has always being available helped me? Well, I grew up in a family with immigrant parents who came here with very little. There was never any room for emotions or my personal concerns. My mom always said, "Tough shit! We don't have the time or money to worry right now, we just have to make it happen." Making it happen has been my mantra all my life. I got lots of attention and love from my parents when I did well in school and didn't have any emotional outbursts. By being available to my team all the time, I've always been able to help solve problems and make sure our team hits our targets. But I've become so hyper-vigilant that over the last fifteen years I've neglected my health and don't have a single hobby or personal interest outside of work and kids. I mean, I guess you could say it's how I got to where I am today, but

I'm not quite sure marinating in anxiety everyday has been worth it. Some days I feel like my heart is going to explode. And not from love.

While the details and circumstances of Andrew's journey may be different than yours, this is a common story for many leaders. In the context of their career, achievement and success is the value that matters most. In a modern world where work takes up the majority of our time and attention, our personal values retreat into the shadows. In *Immunity to Change*, Robert Kegan and Lisa Laskow Lahey describe this as the socialized mind, a process in which we become shaped by the definitions and expectations of our personal environment. As we align ourselves with these expectations, our innate values become secondary and often forgotten. To build a thriving family, we must step back from our social environment to generate an internal seat of judgment. When we do this, we can begin to construct a family that aligns with our own beliefs, ideologies, and personal codes.

As you build your family with your partner, you will be tempted to hide behind your strategic self to avoid conflict. Your family must be a place where everyone's true selves can come home. To create an environment where you and your partner can truly be yourselves, it's important you commit to do three things together:

1. Understand your partner's strategic self and your own. We all have one. We all have learned ways to

compromise our own needs to fit in, avoid conflict, or get something we want. Take the time to share these experiences with your partner and learn about theirs. This will empower you to work as a team.

2. Make an agreement to Stand for Three. Most of the conflict and tension that couples experience results from fighting to protect and legitimize their views of the world and their beliefs about what is right. That is standing for one. Standing for Three means that when you solve problems, you do it in a way that solves for the needs of you, your partner, and the relationship.

3. Speak the truth. As you do the work together, you must be okay with any and all outcomes. Yes, even if that means separation and divorce. It's always the better choice to be honest and single than to compromise your personal values just to stay in a marriage. And please don't get me wrong, I'm not giving you the green light to be an asshole and throw your resentments on your partner. Sharing your truth can be done with humility, grace, and respect.

Although this can be difficult, here's why it matters. Your family is the foundation you lift off of each and every day to make your impact in the world. If you can't experience effortless belonging there, where can you? If you want your family members to bring their gifts to the world, you must create an environment where they feel seen, soothed, secure, supported, and challenged. Creating these conditions for your family all starts with creating them for yourself. If you do this, you will become a transitional character—one who, in a single generation, changes the entire course of your family lineage. Remember, some of the greatest people plant seeds for trees they will never sit under. In doing so, you may just come back home to your true self.

The Next Version of You

In order to evolve into the person you want to become, you must go through a series of experiences that forge that person, experiences that will change how you think and behave in critical moments.

A couple years back I met Todd Herman, a high-performance coach and mental game strategist known around the world for his work helping ambitious entrepreneurs, athletes, and leaders build alter egos to perform under pressure. If you ask me, while sports and business are exciting platforms of performance, there is no field of play that matters more than your family.

If you aren't familiar with the concept of an alter ego, think of Superman. As Todd eloquently explains in his book, *The Alter Ego Effect*, Superman created an alter ego named Clark Kent, a mild-mannered reporter, to blend in and achieve a crucial goal: understanding humans.

The underlying magic of an alter ego is the science of enclothed cognition. A team of researchers out of the University of Minnesota has done a great job of illustrating the power of an alter ego. They gave a bunch of kids a ring of keys, split them into three groups, and put a toy in a locked glass box. The catch? No keys worked. Interested in evaluating how persistent the children were in their efforts to open the box, researchers asked the first control group to open the box. The two other groups were asked to pretend to be Batman or Dora the Explorer. Researchers discovered that when the kids embodied the persona of Batman or Dora, they tried more keys, stayed calm, and worked significantly longer to open the box.

Just as with a professional athlete or a live performer, there are moments that matter when we struggle to turn it on. Moments that make or break our success. Leveraging an alter ego is a performance tactic that allows you to quickly embody the attributes and virtues that are already in you but may not be your default setting under pressure or in moments that matter. Each of us has things we do that we are not proud of, especially at home with our loved ones. And they get in the way of us growing into the person we want to become. You can spend countless years in therapy or personal reflection trying to understand why you do what you do. But even if or when you can figure it out, usually nothing changes. So instead of trying to "figure yourself out," you can take on an alter ego and behave differently when it counts.

Superman's goal was to understand humankind, but your goal is likely going to be different. Maybe you want to be a better listener when your spouse comes to you with problems. Or perhaps you want to control your anger better when your kids are acting out. Or maybe you're a bit like me and want to spend less time on your phone during family time. Regardless of what your intentions are, building an alter ego for yourself will help you accelerate your ability to show up intentionally in difficult moments. And much like anything we deliberately practice, this will become a default way of being.

Now, if you're like most people, your first reaction to the concept of an alter ego is likely "Hmm, this sounds like faking it until you make it," or "Wow, it seems inauthentic to pretend to be someone you aren't." Stay with me. Here is an alternative point of view to consider. Since your earliest memory and throughout your life until now, there have been a million different versions of yourself. In physics terms, you are a wave, not a particle. In Buddhist terms, this is known as "no-self." This means that in every single moment, you have the opportunity to create who you want to be in the next million versions of yourself. The qualities you want to deliberately practice have always been present within you. Using an alter ego is not fake or inauthentic; it is simply a mental performance strategy that leverages the power of your imagination to override your default response. The only thing that is really fake is thinking "I don't know how to manage my anger" or "I don't know how to be direct and give difficult feedback."

Over the last decade, my alter ego, Jacques, has made a profound impact on how I show up at work and at home. I'd love to share this with you to help you understand how to build your own.

As I started to coach professionally, I recognized that I struggled to call bullshit or directly address topics that

I anticipated would create tension or disagreement with a client. In the coaching world, there is a widely held belief that you don't have the answer—your client does. It's your job to ask the right questions to guide your client to their own outcomes. While I agree, I also know there are times when the coach has an obligation to help a client discover the unseen obstacles that are getting in the way of achieving their goals. There were dozens of moments when I would want to confront or challenge my client's perspective on an issue but would find myself allowing him or her to ramble on instead of stepping in. I can remember leaving coaching sessions thinking to myself, "Gahhh, I wish I would've...", only to later learn that my client continued to suffer from the very thing I was afraid to bring up.

It was in these specific moments that I wanted to be more assertive, to the point, calm, and confident. I knew that if I could develop the ability to do this, I would become a much better coach. And my clients weren't the ones making it hard for me to give feedback. It was my own beliefs about what it meant to give someone negative feedback that were creating my anxiety. Remember, you would struggle with all the same things I did if you had all the same experiences—and vice versa.

This is when I built my alter ego, Jacques. There are four key ingredients to creating any alter ego. First, you must have a very specific situation in which you want to perform differently. For me, this was during one-on-one coaching sessions with clients when I felt anxious about confrontation. Next, you have to define what you want to do more or less of in those moments. Instead of keeping the information to myself and validating my client's perspective, I wanted to be more assertive, to the point, and calm, and to confidently bring up a contrary point of view.

The next and most critical ingredient is to identify someone in your life who embodies these qualities. And not just anyone, but someone you have an emotional connection with. So much so that when you think of them, you know exactly how, say, "Sarah your high school basketball coach" would do it. For me, my late grandfather, Jacques, was a living demonstration of respectful assertiveness and calm confidence. Growing up, I always went to Papa when I needed to hear the truth. And while it wasn't always what I wanted to hear, I'll always remember the simple, direct, and kind way he would discuss difficult topics with me.

The other thing you need is a totem: a symbolic object that has significance for you and reminds you of this particular individual. Superman's totem was the black-framed glasses. During his telephone-booth moment, he would put on the glasses to invoke the alter ego and exit as Clark Kent. For me, my totem is an Irish flat cap. For years I have secretly put on this cap before each of my coaching calls. If you look at any of my content on social media, you'll see the exact hat I'm referencing. Every time I put on this hat, I intentionally invoked my alter ego and immediately saw my coaching approach change, just like a little kid putting on a superhero costume.

Over time you are going to benefit from embracing a variety of qualities to be an effective leader with your family. Perhaps you want to embrace the alter ego of a visionary CEO to improve your ability to create a vision for the future, or you want to embody the qualities of an artist to overcome your fear of judgment. Or you want to have more patience when someone is upset, like Mister Rogers would. But what's most important is that you are clear on what behavioral changes would benefit you and your family right now.

Like I mentioned earlier, the journey to building the next version of you and your family is like a spiral staircase. At every step, you have an opportunity to grow and become more authentically you. But you can't change everything in a single step. Your success will come from doing the right next thing after the right next thing after the right next thing. Don't make the mistake of focusing on what your family members need to do to change or make things better. The challenges you are facing with your family are not holding you back from doing more of what you love. They are creating an opportunity for you to grow as a leader. Remember, leading your family is a vehicle for your own personal development. When you focus on you, you will become a lighthouse for your family.

Next Play

Now that you're clear on what brought you here, it's time to start defining where you are going.

1 Get clear on who you want to become

Your family will change you. It's up to you whether they will change you for the better or for the worse, and whether they will bring you closer to your best self or further away. Take a moment to consider these two questions:

1. Who do I want to become?
2. What do I need to learn or experience to become this person?

2 Identify what you need to do differently

To move toward who you want to become, something has to change. You need to do more or less of something in key moments. But you can't change everything at once. Take a moment to journal on these two questions:

1. What would your spouse or kids say their number one complaint about you is?
2. What do you know you need to do, but for whatever reason you haven't been able to do consistently?

3 Build an alter ego

Take a few moments to start capturing the key ingredients:

1. What is the situation you want to show up differently in?
2. What do you want to do more or less of?
3. Who in your life is a great example of this?
4. What totem can you use to invoke your alter ego?
5. What is your alter ego's name?

3

It's Not What You Look at That Matters, It's What You See

IF YOU walk into my kitchen, in addition to finding the aftermath of a toddler hurricane and the wake of two teenagers, you will find a blue sticky note on the fridge door that reads, "It's not what you look at that matters, it's what you see."

I can recall the day it was ripped from the stack of freshly opened Post-its and slapped onto the fridge. Jen and I were right in the middle of the most challenging and argumentative time in our marriage to date. The placement of this sticky note was a proclamation from Jen, in an attempt to remind me that I had a choice to see what I wanted to see in the situation we were in. I like to snack, so her placement was clearly strategic. I'm surprised there weren't others stuck to my mountain bike and tennis bag.

Jen will be the first to tell you how good I am at "making it right." You probably know someone who does this really well; regardless of the issue, it is quickly transformed into an opportunity to shine or explain the circumstances to justify what did or didn't happen. Moments before placing this sticky note on our fridge, Jen had been reminding me how good I am at doing this for myself and atrocious at doing it for her. And she was right. But I didn't want to see it at the time. Looking back, I was in a bit of a rut. A few months before this, Jen had given birth to her third child and my first: William. At this time in our life, I was the only one working, while Jen was on maternity leave with William. When I came home from work, I would become frustrated with Jen for the lack of visible effort she put into the house while I was busy working. Every dirty counter, toy on the ground, pile of dirty laundry, or piece of garbage in the car was proof that I was right. I was keeping score, and resentment was on the rise.

Predictive disgust from a place of superiority is one of the leading predictors of divorce. It's when you look out in the future and make decisions about someone's intentions before you have evidence that anything has happened. And boy was I good at it. World-renowned relationship expert Dr. John Gottman explains this well: "When contempt begins to overwhelm your relationship, you tend to forget entirely your partner's positive qualities, at least while you're feeling upset. You can't remember a single positive quality or act." My myopic view and the resulting contempt for Jen had our relationship on a fast track to separation. This is not an uncommon experience during the early days of parenthood—again, sucks but normal. My default in conflict is to avoid and create space from the situation. So naturally, my Google history would have shown you that I was already in the process of looking for a new place to live.

The things you give attention and energy to will grow. And the more you pay attention to them, the more you see them. Every day the list of things Jen wasn't doing got bigger and bigger.

The illusion here is something called the Baader-Meinhof phenomenon, a type of frequency bias that explains how your awareness of something increases to the point where you believe something is happening more, even if that's not the case. This happened to me not too long ago when we purchased a new truck. Once we picked it up, I could have sworn everyone on the road was also driving a Chevrolet Traverse. What gives?

Because I was so sure I was doing more than Jen, my brain was searching for data to validate this perspective, even if that meant overlooking and ignoring all the things she was doing. In fact, not only was I searching for all the work she didn't do, but my awareness of extra work that I could do to amplify the imbalance expanded too. When we don't explicitly define what matters to us, our emotional needs and pain will make this decision for us.

I've had to learn this lesson several times in my life. During the early stages of starting my first business, the

Concussion Toolbox, the only scoreboard I was keeping track of was revenue and personal income. The unseen obstacle for me at the time was that I was deeply connecting my sense of self-worth to my net worth. And relative to my peers, I didn't have enough. So I just worked more! In my case, I kept doing this until my wakeup call when my girlfriend left me.

Ultimately, my insatiable hunger for money created the paradigm I used to experience the world. And the lens we view the world through informs the things we do and ultimately shapes the results we experience. Stephen Covey illustrates this beautifully with his See-Do-Get Cycle. The way we *see* the world (paradigm) informs the things we *do* (behavior) and creates the results we *get* (outcome). While most people are infatuated with productivity hacks, the most effective leaders understand that great change comes from altering the paradigm with which they experience the world. When you really *get* this, it's a big idea that will change your life and the way you solve problems.

So let me offer you a new paradigm for leading your family—and yourself.

The B-Corporation

Just after my girlfriend left me back in 2013, I went to Hawaii all by myself for a week. After seven days of solitude and self-reflection, I hopped on my flight back home knowing that my paradigm needed a shakeup.

Now, maybe you're one of those people who hate talking to others on a plane. Noise-canceling headphones, a cold beer, and a package of tasteless cookies is all you need for a smooth flight. Not me. As a heartbroken extrovert who had just spent a week alone talking to myself about some of life's existential questions, I was thirsty for conversation on the way home. God bless whoever was going to sit down beside me for the six-hour flight to Denver before I carried on to Toronto.

Once we got up in the air, my neighbor Andrew and I quickly struck up a conversation and started to share details from our trips. When asked about my experience, I couldn't help but share the personal journey I was on. Both being entrepreneurs, we immediately connected over our innate thirst for autonomy and desire to create our own way of doing things. Shortly after the flight attendant came by with dinner, I remember saying to Andrew, "Man, I just feel like one of those big mining companies that makes great profits but leaves a trail of destruction." In the wake of my recent separation, I was disappointed that I had allowed my new business to cast such a large shadow on so many important things in my life.

With a mouth half-filled with food, Andrew quietly asked, "Well... have you ever heard of a B-corporation?"

"A B-corporation? What the hell is that?" I asked.

Over the next hour, I learned about B-corporations and how they were changing the way leaders were doing business around the world. If you've never heard of them before, B-corporations, aka benefit corporations, were created in the 1990s as a new breed of businesses committed to making profit *and* a positive impact in the world through responsible and values-based leadership.

You don't have to look far for examples of organizations or entire industries that are focused on creating profit and shareholder value at all costs. The rechargeable batteries in your electric car, iPhone, and laptop are a great example of this. One of the key ingredients in lithium ion batteries is cobalt. Today, dozens of international mining companies operate in southern Congo, where almost half of the world's known supply of cobalt is found. While executive teams around the world strategize on how to meet the market demand for their products, there are thousands of miners in Congo who show up to work every day to dig by hand. Children too. While shareholders collect their dividends, workers in the remote landscape of central Africa return home with barely enough money to provide their families with food. Not to mention the regular loss of life from collapsing tunnels and poor working conditions.

It's heartbreaking, but it shouldn't be a surprise to anyone. Corporations are designed to maximize revenue and profit for shareholders. It's in their DNA. Again, what we measure and give our attention to grows. When the bottom line is your scoreboard, you tend to make decisions at the cost of other important resources, such as people or the planet.

On the opposite end of the spectrum, you have non-profits, which are registered charities that are tax exempt and have a mandate to make a positive social impact and public benefit, often on a shoestring budget that is laughable at the best of times.

B-corporations create a third option. I personally love this because, as an entrepreneur, it allows me to have both a capital and a social mission. To have my cake and eat it too. Why not both, right?

I'll be honest. At first I thought the concept of B-corporations was just a branding exercise to embellish companies' efforts in a masquerade of "doing good." Greenwashing, for example: marketing products and services as sustainable when they are actually not. Shortly after returning home from Hawaii, I started to do some research to satisfy my bullshit detector. My first question was, "So who are these B-corporations anyways?"

As it turns out, they were TOMS Shoes, Allbirds, Patagonia, Ben & Jerry's, the Business Development Bank of Canada, the Body Shop... all corporations that I knew about. In fact, I was a customer of many B-corporations but had no idea about their commitment to "Not Business as Usual." Maybe this explained why Ben & Jerry's ice cream tastes so good? I knew I could taste love in there.

B-corporations are the real deal and operate in a variety of industries around the world. To become a B-corporation, you must explicitly set up a formal legal structure, management systems, and by-laws to remain accountable and steadfast in your commitment to social and environmental goals, in addition to profit. And there is one management framework that is common to all B-corporations: the triple bottom line.

The Triple Bottom Line

The triple bottom line is a management framework that illustrates a B-corporation's holistic approach to success, where people, planet, and profit are factored into all decision making and management.

- **People:** social responsibility, community involvement, special benefits for staff and families, and equitable and equal opportunities
- **Planet:** conservation and carbon neutrality programs, recycling initiatives, sustainable material sourcing, supply chain optimization, tree planting, and animal welfare
- **Profit:** maximizing growth, creating new revenue streams, and creating cashflow to fund missions

I bet you're a bit like me. For me, success has never been *just* about money. I remember reclining my chair on the flight home from Hawaii and writing at the top of my journal, "There are non-traditional currencies that are worth building wealth in." This simple yet profound paradigm for managing a company gave me the language to describe something that has always felt right to me. Instead of planet and people being "costs of doing business," they could become a design constraint in how profit was generated. I'd had the right *high-level* gameplan, but I'd never had an *eye-level* strategy or practice to make sure I followed through on the things I said I would. In the absence of a clear strategy, I was drifting toward what either made me feel good or made me money. But in the process, I wasn't seeing or experiencing the things that really mattered to me: strong and meaningful relationships, or the health and vitality I knew I needed to lead for the long term.

After Andrew and I chatted for a while longer, he decided to watch a movie, and I opened my journal to reflect on a few things.

I Have the Skills
The first thing I reflected on was that I am very good at creating space to regularly define and refine strategy to win in my business. I effectively use frameworks like "Where to Play, How to Win" and objectives and key results to mobilize teams and focus efforts. This has been an essential part of going through the new venture creation process, and more importantly, it's a key ingredient for any business to thrive and win in the long term.

Yet, there I was, humbled to realize that I was failing to do that for my most important enterprise: my life and family. At the time, I didn't have any kids. But even then, I wasn't leading the family I did have—or myself, for that matter.

The good news was that I had the skills to do this. I just needed to apply them in a different way. And so do you.

I Have Been Stealing
Looking back, I had talked a big game, but my audio wasn't matching my video. I said that relationships mattered to me, yet I would cancel a dinner date or movie

night with my partner to take a customer call without hesitation. Or even worse, when we were together, I would be checking my email all the time, pretending I was able to do both.

When starting something new or going through significant change, you quite often have to borrow time or money to make it happen. However, borrowing is predicated on a shared agreement between two parties, often with a promise to repay. I wasn't borrowing time from my family and friends. I was stealing it.

How Might We...?

The principle of a triple bottom line makes a lot of sense and, if nothing else, provides a holistic lens for making values-based decisions about how to operate an organization. I loved how the triple bottom line challenged leaders to find ways to grow profit while making a positive impact on people and the planet. And not from a place of obligation. Instead, people and planet were seen as design constraints.

So, how might we apply the concept of a triple bottom line to a leader's personal life and family?

Your Family's Triple Bottom Line

Much like in a business, we can assume that profit or personal wealth is going to be a primary focus for your triple bottom line. But if planet and people were the non-traditional currencies of a B-corporation, what would two non-traditional currencies be for your family and life?

When I started to think about this, I immediately thought about *time*. But the reality is, you can't create more time. Everyone has 168 hours in their week, or 1,440 minutes in a day. For something to qualify as a currency, we must be able to grow it, or else what is the purpose of it being on the bottom line? If you're interested in strategies to get more value from your time, go and read *Buy Back Your Time* by Dan Martell. It's a great how-to, especially for executives and entrepreneurs. But when it comes to your triple bottom line, I would encourage you to see time as an input function. You must become a master of it, but time is not the scoreboard you should be measuring. We'll talk more about this in future chapters.

Hungry to define my own triple bottom line, I started meeting with and studying remarkable leaders like Dr. Greg Wells, Dr. James Rouse, Robin Sharma, Marianne Williamson, John Maxwell, and many more. While the result was a whole constellation of interesting answers and discussions, it was clear that leaders who were high-performing and highly fulfilled had two things in common: they all had great health and strong relationships.

Health

Here's a big idea. If you want to be an icon in your industry and experience tremendous success, live longer than your competitors.

You've heard it before, but I'll say it again for the people in the back or those with thicker skulls: health is wealth and is a mission-critical resource for competing in and contributing to the world. A healthy woman may have many wishes, but an unhealthy woman has only one.

While I completely respect that each of us has unique genetic predispositions to various ailments, the investments we make in our mental, emotional, physical, and spiritual well-being are within our circle of influence and have a direct impact on the capacity and resilience we have to lead in this world.

While there are over 8 billion examples of ways people spend their lives, there are generally two types of people: those who sacrifice health to achieve success, and those who intentionally invest in their health and leverage it as a competitive advantage to win.

And what has one of the greatest impacts on your health and quality of life? Relationships.

Relationships

In the 1940s, a group of researchers at Harvard University started the Harvard Study of Adult Development, also known as the Grant Study. At the core of this collective effort was one important question: "What makes a good life?"

Turns out, it doesn't matter how much wine you drink, how many times you exercise per week, or the amount of sleep you get. The Grant Study taught us that relationships are by far the strongest predictor of life satisfaction. In fact, strong relationships were highly correlated with physical health, longevity, and financial success. So, not only do relationships improve the quality of your life, but they also will contribute to the growth of your overall triple bottom line.

It's easy to make the mistake of using your number of friends as a vanity metric for the current state of your relationships. But unlike your Instagram account, we are *not* looking for quantity here. When it comes to relationships, what we are truly aiming for is something I mentioned in Chapter 2: effortless belonging.

For centuries, great philosophers and mystics have described effortless belonging as the pinnacle of consciousness, something we are all called to experience. If you ask me, effortless belonging is all about marinating in the presence of love and acceptance without laboring to fit in or maintain a certain expectation. At the end of the day, this is what it means to win. I hope you are lucky enough to experience this.

COVID was a potent reminder of how we've taken community for granted. We know that social isolation significantly increases a person's risk of premature death from all causes and is associated with higher rates of depression, anxiety, and suicide. Relationships with others are fundamental to our well-being. But even more so is our relationship with self. The depth of your relationships with others will never exceed the depth of your relationship with yourself.

A few weeks after Jen placed the Post-it on the fridge, we had one of our Family Basecamps (more to come on this in Chapter 8), where we regroup and check in on our triple bottom line. During this time together, it dawned on me that while Jen may not have been working and contributing to our household income, she was doing an amazing job taking care of our family's health and relationships. I had made a fundamental attribution error: in my mind, if I forgot to clean up the kitchen after making lunch, it was because I was in a rush to join an important meeting, but when Jen forgot to clean up, it was because she was a lazy slob who was treating maternity leave like vacation. The causes of my shortcomings were always circumstantial, while hers were deeply connected to her character. Until I looked at our situation through the paradigm of the triple bottom line, I didn't see it.

You've likely made that mistake too. Permission to be human. That is why it is so important to have a shared framework to keep you clear-headed and focused on what's important. Instead of keeping score about who does what, use the triple bottom line as your family scoreboard—something you are working together to grow over time.

Your Starting Line

Before you start building your family by design, we need to establish your baseline to help you get clear on where to begin and what to focus on. To do this, I'd like to teach you how to evaluate your triple bottom line.

It doesn't matter how good or bad your triple bottom line is right now. What matters most is your ability to be brutally honest about your current reality. Because when we can harness intellectual humility and acknowledge exactly where we are, we create the opportunity to make a choice—a choice to either do nothing or make the change we want to see.

I teach leaders how to reflect on their triple bottom line using a four-star evaluation. It's simple and to the point, and it helps you quickly conduct a check-in to identify the key areas to focus on going forward.

If you rate yourself *one star*, this means

- you are experiencing poverty in this area of your life; and
- the lack of resources is a blocker to you performing well, or at all.

Next step: Acknowledge reality, then get the help you need to figure out the right next step.

If you rate yourself *two stars*, this means

- you know what you should be doing, but you aren't doing it; and
- the investments you are making are inconsistent.

Next step: Focus on finding ways to change your behaviors and form sustainable healthy habits.

If you rate yourself *three stars*, this means

- you know what you should be doing, and you're doing it; and
- you are experiencing positive results from your efforts and experiencing growth.

Next step: Focus on finding ways to be more effective and efficient.

If you rate yourself *four stars*, this means

- you have enough resources in this area of your life to share it with others; and
- you are empowering others to grow their health, wealth, and/or relationships.

Next step: Buy back your time and uncover opportunities to leverage your resources to take on more.

People don't remember facts, they remember stories. So I want to share a few with you to illustrate each level of wealth using this four-star evaluation tool. I can promise you that none of these stories will perfectly represent your situation. The aim is to use these anecdotes to help you accurately evaluate yourself.

One Star in Wealth: Jordan, Startup Founder

Over the last five years I have started seven different companies, none of them successful. I like to say that the money I spent trying to start each business was the equivalent to my real-life MBA. About twelve months ago I took on $150,000 in investment from a small group of angel investors and family and friends. Aiming to build an influencer marketing SAAS product, I hired a small team of engineers and worked heads down for six months. About sixty days ago we ran out of money and I had to start taking on side consulting projects to try to cover the businesses expenses. I haven't taken a personal paycheck in three months and have burned through my life savings along the way. I've unfortunately started to take on credit card debt to pay for our family expenses and had *to cancel our upcoming family vacation. Our two kids were pretty pissed. And so am I. I am not even sure what to do next. I feel like I'm barely treading water.*

This is what it looks like to rate one star in your wealth. The lack of financial resources and income in Jordan's life not only are holding his company back but have put him at a point where he is unable to pay his family's monthly expenses. Jordan is overwhelmed with stress and unable to describe a clear path forward. At his wits' end, Jordan is exhausted and unaware of the next step he should take.

Two Stars in Health: Debra, Corporate Executive

About six months ago I slipped and got a concussion while heading out the door to grab the mail. I tried to return to work about a month ago after taking some time off, but I just can't seem to shake my symptoms. By the time lunch comes around, I don't have any energy left. Most days that means I don't even get to the recovery exercises my physiotherapist prescribed. When I did them regularly, it made such a big difference, but after attending a handful of client meetings and spending a few hours on emails, I am gassed. What I really need to do is have a meeting with my boss to find a better way to have consistent times throughout the day to take breaks and get my rehab in.

They say knowledge is power, but that is a lie. Application of knowledge is where the real magic happens. Debra's story illustrates what it means to rate two stars in health. Unlike someone who rates one star, Debra knows what she needs to do for her recovery, but she isn't doing it. Her next step is to focus on becoming more consistent and overcoming the obstacles getting in the way.

Three Stars in Relationships:
Jeremy, Non-profit Executive Director

I've been using the triple bottom line to think about my family for the last few years, and it has completely changed my relationships. My partner Andrea and I play a ton of golf together throughout the year. We have realized that with the kids getting older, playing sports together is one of the most fun ways for us to have one-on-one time together and stay healthy. And we continue to go on a date night together every week. For the kids, I coach both of their basketball teams, and we love the time we have together heading to and from the games. It's a great opportunity to bond as a family. I also take each kid out of school for one day every semester to have one-on-one time with them. It's the highlight of my month usually. And my parents, well, they are getting quite a bit older now. For the last few months, I've been going by my parents' place every other weekend to cut the lawn, clean up the yard, and fix anything that is broken or needs some TLC. While my parents obviously love the help, I know that more than anything they love having lunch together and catching up when I'm done.

The first thing that should stand out to you is *clarity*. Jeremy has a remarkable level of clarity about how and where he is investing time and energy. And it's working for him. The time, energy, and money he is investing in his relationships are generating a positive return. His focus going forward is on making these investments easier and increasing the quantity of time spent building each relationship. If Jeremy wanted to grow his relationship score from three to four, he would be focused on creating opportunities to share his relationships with others or to help others make new ones.

Four Stars in Health: Jessica, Director of Communications

I used to love doing adventure races and was lucky enough to meet the love of my life, Mark, at one of the events. Our shared love for endurance sport quickly grew into a love for each other. About five years ago, Mark and I really got into Ironman racing. Mark is an incredible coach, and all of the hard work we did together during COVID led to me winning Ironman Canada in 2022. It was crazy. Over the last year we've grown a community of fifty endurance athletes who are eager to learn and grow from us. It's been really cool to participate in the success of other athletes and create a community that can push us and them to become world-class.

This is a great example of someone who has four stars in health. Jessica not only actively invests in her own health and well-being, but through her success and commitment has created an endurance training club to empower others to grow their own health and relationships. By focusing on challenging others to invest in their health, Jessica creates the opportunity to explore advanced training opportunities.

The triple bottom line is a way for you, the Chief Family Officer, to assess how your family invests their time, energy, and money. I've taught hundreds of leaders how to use a triple bottom line with their family, and there are always a handful of leaders who ask one of two questions: 1) Can I use currencies other than health and relationships? and 2) Do I focus on improving all three areas at once?

When it comes to using other currencies for your triple bottom line, here's my advice: Adopt it, then adapt it. Start with the framework and tools I have provided and use them for at least six months. Once you've built the foundation and practice of using a triple bottom line, adapt the model to suit your own values and focus.

And where to start? The reality is, growth and change take a lot of energy. After evaluating your family's triple bottom line, select one currency you want to intentionally improve and grow, and just start there. I would much rather see you make progress and build momentum in one area than struggle to get traction in two or three at the same time.

Next Play

Before you embark on change, it's always wise to establish a baseline of where you are today. Take a few moments to evaluate your triple bottom line, and identify the most important currency for you and your family to focus on next.

1 Evaluate your personal triple bottom line

1. What is the current balance of your personal triple bottom line: wealth, health, and relationships?

2. What is the most important currency for you to focus on for the next six to twelve weeks?

3. What is the most important problem for you to solve and overcome?

2 Evaluate the triple bottom line of your family and discuss with your partner

1. What is the current balance of your family's triple bottom line?

2. What is the most important currency for your family to focus on over the next six to twelve weeks?

3. What is the most important problem for you to solve and overcome?

4

Playing to Win

I COULD SENSE the looming presence of someone waiting behind me, like that awkward feeling you get when someone is watching you, as I took a quick sip of water while zipping up my bag. I turned and saw Claire, president of a regional insurance brokerage.

"Hey! Amazing session today," she said. "It really hit home with me. Any chance I can take you out to dinner while you're in town?"

For the previous three hours I had led a private session with around thirty executives and business owners from a regional CEO forum in Edmonton, Alberta. I could tell there was something personal on Claire's mind that she was hesitant to bring up in front of the group.

"Sure! Why don't you join me for a bite to eat this evening?" I asked. Luckily I already had reservations downtown at an upscale steakhouse.

I stopped back by my hotel to freshen up and answer some emails, then headed over to the restaurant. As the server was pouring me a glass of wine, Claire joined me at the table. "Thanks so much for agreeing to share dinner together!" she said as she sat down. "Your story helped me understand how I've been messing up over the last few years."

Over the next fifteen minutes, Claire told me how her husband had recently shared that he had fallen out of love and didn't want to be married anymore. With three young boys now entering their teenage years, the last five years had been wild. Between two busy careers, a full house renovation, a job change, a calendar filled with kids' activities, and a middle child struggling with self-harm and suicidal ideation, their relationship had slipped into the shadows. Claire was blindsided and had no idea their relationship had been hanging on by such a thin thread. Their impending separation happened gradually, and then suddenly.

I asked her, "What do you imagine your husband's biggest complaint about you is right now?"

Claire leaned forward on her left elbow as her eyes welled up with tears. "Oh my gosh, where do I begin? He would probably say that my desire to take on so much has led to our family feeling completely overwhelmed and exhausted. After I took over my father's business four years ago, he really stepped up to make sure the boys always got their homework done, made it to sports on time, doctor's appointments, et cetera, so I could put in some extra time at work to get things under control.

Over the years, conversations about this type of stuff always led to arguments, so we just avoided it... until we couldn't. His biggest complaint would be how our family's life revolves around me, and there is no room for his interests."

"Claire, let me ask you. What does it mean for your family to win?"

Claire's silence was her answer. As I sat back and patiently waited for her answer, I could tell she had no idea what it meant for her family to win. And if she didn't, then there was no chance in hell her husband and boys knew what it meant. There was no uniting vision connecting her family and guiding their decisions together.

I flipped over her napkin and grabbed a pen from my pocket. "I want you to write down three numbers. On a scale of 1 to 10, rate how clear you are on what it means for your business to win, what it means for you to win personally, and what it means for your family to win, together?"

In no time at all, Claire scribbled her numbers and flipped it around:

"8—9—2"

The Power of Creating Context

Whether you're leading a business or your family, strategy creates the context and container for a team to thrive, struggle, and adapt together. If you don't have a united vision, your team will gradually drift apart and remain focused on the vision they have for themselves. And every strategy starts and ends with a clear definition of what it means to win. Just imagine building a home without a blueprint. Do you think you'd be proud of the final product if you were figuring it out as you went?

Many teams make the mistake of looking for a tactic or hack for what is really a strategy problem. Improve your time management and communication skills all you want, but if you don't decide what it means to win, you will never have a unifying vision to guide your efforts and decision making. You will be driven by infatuation instead of intention.

Perhaps you have an old definition or vision that no longer fits your situation. Or maybe you've never built one. Either way, winning must be explicitly defined and understood by everyone! As a Chief Family Officer, it is your job to make this happen.

One of my mentors, Philip McKernan, often says, "Those who only look forward are blind." Looking back can be quite helpful at times. It helps us witness behaviors and patterns that may not be obvious moment to moment. However, spending excess time trying to make sense of the past is also one of the leading complaints from couples who don't get results from going to therapy or counseling together. Whether you're leading a business, yourself, or a family, your growth depends on your ability to look into the past and the future.

Many couples are waiting for their partner to get better at communication, be more present with the kids, or discover better ways to manage conflict. And until that changes, they are unwilling to talk about the future. My experience has taught me that a shared definition of what it means to win *together* is a missing puzzle piece holding them back from having a shared reason to work together on something like communication or conflict resolution. When you define what it means to win, you create a reason for the both of you to work together. And instead of waiting for your partner to change, you can allow their changes to take place in pursuit of your vision together. Instead of doing it for you, they have a reason to do it for themselves. Because let's not forget, people do things for their reasons, not yours. Defining what it means to win also creates context for answering important questions like "Are we living in the right neighborhood?" "Should I take this job?" "Is now the right time to start this business?" or "Should we buy this new car?"

When it comes to building a winning strategy, Roger Martin is one of the best in the business. He clearly delineates the difference between strategy and planning. When it comes to strategy, Roger emphasizes the following:

1. Strategy is about making choices. To win, you must choose to do some things and not others.

2. Strategy is about increasing the odds of success. There is no such thing as a *perfect* strategy.

3. Successful strategy-making combines both rigor and creativity.

Now, you may be thinking that building a family strategy is overkill because at the end of the day, shit happens and life unfolds as it does. You're not wrong, but you're not right either. In *The 7 Habits of Highly Effective Families*, Stephen Covey stresses how critical "Bringing Purpose and Vision to Your Family" is to constructing a blueprint for your family to thrive.

> What I have observed over and over is that families who do have a clear sense of vision, values, and direction accomplish significantly more than families who do not. Life isn't always easy for these families, but it is easier for them than it would be if they were adrift aimlessly with no solid goals or values to anchor them.

When it came to her business and career, Claire could easily describe what it meant to win. But her family? Not quite as easy. In fact, as I would soon learn through our conversations, Claire was far clearer on what it meant to lose. Both Claire and her husband were in survival mode, overwhelmed with anxiety and anger from being misaligned and avoiding important conversations.

Without a clear family strategy, Claire and her husband were fighting for their own unmet needs, arguing to get the other person to legitimize and understand their experience. By going back to the fundamentals of strategy, Claire and her husband could create a context for their relationship and, instead of fighting against each other (me versus you), sit on the same side of the table to begin exploring possibilities and making important life choices (us versus it). Choices as simple as "Should we sign up the boys for hockey *and* indoor soccer this year?" and as complicated and critical as "Is now a good time for me to take over my father's business?" or "Should we stay together?"

Making Strategic Choices

As we wrapped up dinner together, Claire asked, "How do I save my marriage?" To which I responded, "Is it a marriage worth saving? Can you win together?"

Over the years, your family will cross many significant thresholds: moments where everything changes. Getting married, the birth of a child, moving to a new place, starting a new job, losing a loved one, or kids moving out on their own. A new threshold was crossed when Claire's husband shared his desire to separate. When we cross thresholds, it is critical to re-evaluate your family strategy. To figure out if her marriage was worth saving, Claire needed to focus on understanding what it meant for her to win, for her husband to win, and for their family to win together. Getting clear on this would help them both decide if they could win together, or not.

As we finished dinner, I instructed Claire to work with her husband to answer three important questions:

1. What does it mean for us to win?
2. Where will we play?
3. How will we win together?

1 What Does It Mean for Us to Win?

The external marketplace is always changing. And same with your internal marketplace—the needs, capacity, and desires of your family members. As Chief Family Officer, you must focus on staying attuned and adaptable to your family needs. Instead of working to find the *best* strategy, focus on looking for opportunities to make it *better* over time. Quite often when I work with couples, one of the individuals wants to build a vision for where they are going in the future, but the other is reluctant to have the conversation because they are so frustrated with how things are today. "You want to talk about the future? Ha, good one. I've been asking you for years to become more present with me and the kids when you are at home, and nothing's changed. How about you fix that, and then we can start talking about tomorrow." Like I said in Chapter 1, one of the biggest challenges you are going to have to overcome in this work is the desire for your partner to change. Crafting a unifying vision for your family will provide your family members with a reason to change. Because as I illustrated when I discussed goals in Chapter 2, if the motivation to change is to stop the nagging and criticism, the motivation to do the work will go away as soon as the original source of pain is gone.

As you lean into vision work, it is important that you build a vision over multiple horizons. One of the best ways to do this is to think about winning as a family now, next, and when.

Horizon 1: What does it mean for us to win right now?
An effective strategy must be aligned with the unique opportunities and challenges your family is facing today. Think about the next zero to twelve months, and ask yourself this:

- What is our family's highest priority goal?
- What is the right next thing for us to focus on as a family?

In some situations, winning means going on offense and working together to strive for a big hairy audacious goal such as helping your kid earn an athletic scholarship to a Division 1 school, selling a family business, or taking a year sabbatical to explore the corners of the earth.

And at times, you may need to play a bit of defense, regain control, and focus on getting back to the basics. Remember, you are only as good as your *least well* family member. According to the World Health Organization, around 450 million people are currently struggling with mental illness. In Canada, where my family lives, one in two Canadians has—or has had—a mental illness by the time they reach forty years of age. At some point in your journey as a Chief Family Officer, winning will mean nurturing the well-being and safety of those you love.

It's cool if you can build a big vision of what it means to win, but if it isn't connected to reality, you are delusionally optimistic and failing to align your strategy with the honest reality of your situation. If you don't, you run the risk of worsening a situation with more pressure and intensity. At times you are going to need to adapt and make adjustments. This might be for three months, or three years. This hard work requires your leadership. Everyone's definition of winning is going to be relative.

Once you've gotten clear on what winning means *right now*, then you can begin exploring the second horizon.

Horizon 2: What does it mean for us to win over the next one to three years?

Horizon 2 is all about anticipating the next chapter of your family's journey. As Wayne Gretzky has famously said, "Skate to where the puck is going, not where it has been." As a Chief Family Officer, you must do both simultaneously. Whether you're a business or a family, you can remain adaptable and thrive during change if you simultaneously remain clear on what winning means today and tomorrow. When you are thinking about Horizon 2, ask yourself these questions:

- What do we want to be celebrating one to three years from now?
- How do we want to be experiencing life day to day?

Once you've built a vision for *now* and *next*, it's time to look even further out in the future and start dreaming unapologetically.

Horizon 3: What will it mean to win when...?

Every family crosses thresholds in life. Moments when everything is different. Horizon 3 starts with understanding what your family is waiting for. This is when you can begin dreaming about life after a significant threshold you are anticipating five or more years from now. For example:

- What does it mean to win when *we sell our family business?*
- What does it mean to win when *our kids move out?*
- What does it mean to win when *our parents move into elder care?*
- What does it mean to win when *we are no longer caregivers for our parents?*

As I write this book, our kids are fifteen, thirteen, and three years old. Our Horizon 3 is when the big kids graduate high school and move out to college or university. For us, it is a threshold where our commitments and responsibilities as parents will significantly change. It will have a big impact on our ability to travel and our flexibility in where we live. It will also unlock a significant amount of time and energy for both Jen and me.

Once you have identified the upcoming threshold in your life, you can start to dream unapologetically about what life could be like. Where would you like to live? What would you like to be doing for work? What does your community look like? How are you investing in your health and well-being? How do you spend your free time?

The big idea here is that it is important to define what winning means over multiple time horizons. Horizon 1 (now) is all about what it means to win today. This provides the clarity to align everyone on your day-to-day decision making and informs how you schedule your time and energy. Horizon 2 (next) is all about what's coming around the corner. Your definition of winning here becomes something you are constantly thinking about as your next destination. And Horizon 3 (when) is all about transformation when you reach the threshold that's coming on your horizon, where your life will change significantly.

2 Where Will We Play?

"I think I might have decided to start my business at the wrong time, Dave."

One of my favorite things to do is catch up with old friends on the phone when I am out for a walk with my dog, Mango. During one of those calls, my friend Michael confessed to me that he was feeling overwhelmed by the reality of his decision to quit his job and start a new business while parenting two kids under the age of three. While he was doing his best to be a present parent and partner, the pressure to earn a paycheck month to month was eating at him from the inside out. Through our conversation, it dawned on him that starting a business and becoming an entrepreneur was a part of what it meant for him to win, but it was grossly misaligned with what it meant for his family to win over the next couple years. He was in a pickle—a common issue that arises after making decisions for yourself when you aren't clear on what it means for your family to win together.

Once you understand what it means to win, you become empowered to evaluate where you are playing today and to make strategic decisions about where you want to play tomorrow. In order to win, you are going to have to invest time and energy to make it happen. Where to play is all about the vehicles that will take you forward. When thinking about where to play, there are generally three areas that will have a profound impact on your success: 1) where you live, 2) where you work, and 3) who you hang out with.

Take a moment to think about your family's triple bottom line.

When it comes to your health goals and aspirations, what gyms and programs are your family members enrolled in to improve your fitness and your mental health? For relationships, what communities do you belong to, and who is your inner circle? For wealth, what type of career are you earning a living from, and what investments are you making to grow your capital?

Once you capture a draft of where you are playing *currently*, it's time to audit your existing commitments to evaluate how aligned your family is with your winning aspiration. I love to use the traffic light model as a simple means of evaluating alignment.

You can evaluate each point by reflecting on three things for each family member:

1. Does it align with and support your family's winning aspiration?
2. Do you want to play there?
3. Is the place you play working well and making a positive impact?

Green: You answer "yes" to all three questions.

Yellow: You answer "yes" to two of the questions.

Red: You answer "yes" to one or none of the questions.

These types of conversations are best kept for you and your spouse to have privately. As with a great business partnership, it's important to get on the same page about strategic issues before sharing them with the broader team. Same goes for your family.

As you discuss where your family is current playing, it's important to consider

- what's missing;
- what is no longer serving them; and
- what is working really well.

Playing in the right areas is critical to winning as a family. In fact, deciding where to play has the single greatest influence on whether or not you will succeed individually and as a family. Every family's situation and circumstances will be unique, but here are three of the most common core issues that surface.

1. **You are playing in the wrong place.**
   For many families, the biggest thing holding them back is continuing to play in a place that is no longer serving them. For example, a family may have the desire to spend significant parts of the year traveling, yet the parents have jobs that require them to work in an office forty-plus hours a week. Or perhaps the

school your kids are going to is not set up to support their academic aspirations and challenges. As a Chief Family Officer, it's important you are always reflecting on the "fit" and if it is serving you and your family.

2. **You are playing in too many places at once.**
I rarely meet families who are underwhelmed. Between school, work, after-school commitments, sports, family time, grocery shopping, laundry... most families have normalized operating beyond their capacity. At times, there is a breaking point where your family may be playing in too many areas at once. Remember, all things trend toward disorder. Over time, the scope of our commitments creeps until we gradually and then quite suddenly feel overwhelmed and unable to focus on the things that really matter. As a Chief Family Officer, you must always be monitoring the bandwidth of your family and uncovering opportunities to simplify the way things get done.

3. **You are not playing in the areas you should be.**
After defining what it means to win, many families recognize they lack meaningful opportunities to do things together as a family. Upon reflecting on "where everyone is playing," it is quite common for families to realize that they are winning individually, but there are very few commitments that bring them together as a team. It is important that both happen simultaneously. Your family members can win individually and together as a family at the same time. But it doesn't happen by chance.

3 How Will We Win Together?

There is always more than one way to win. If you audit your current commitments and feel like everything is well aligned... good for you! Celebrate this, and make a commitment to check back in six to twelve months from now. But if you're like most people, this process should illuminate a handful of changes you can make to get realigned and back on the pathway to winning. When you make changes to a business model, we call this a pivot. These changes come in the form of either macro-changes or micro-changes.

Macro-changes are when you make a decision to fundamentally change "where you play" to better align with your winning aspiration as a family—changes such as where you work, where you live, what school your kids go to, the club they play sports at, the advisors you work with, the company you keep, and the communities you belong to.

When it comes to making macro-changes, there are two important concepts to consider. First, define your constraints. The reality is that you may be limited in your options to make macro-changes due to circumstance. For example, you may have aging parents in town, limited disposable income, or kids with deeply entrenched relationships through sports or school. Your work may not have the flexibility to let you work part-time for three to six months to prioritize supporting a child who is struggling in school or with their mental health. It's important to identify these as constraints and begin to solve for how to win in that reality. For example, if you can't go down to a part-time job and reduce your income, reframe the question to ask, "How might we work full-time jobs and spend more quality time with our child who is struggling with their mental health?" Strong leaders always reframe problems as opportunities.

A second important concept is to challenge your assumptions. Change is almost always met with resistance and bullshit excuses. The bigger the perceived change, the bigger the resistance. As you consider macro-changes, you may be met with thoughts such as "They would never let me work remotely for six months so we can travel to South America," or "My kids would never want to leave their friends and move to a new school." Be careful of these assumptions. Instead of accepting them as truth, be curious and ask others to explore the possibility with you. If you keep these worries and fears in your head, you're dead. Build a list and stare at them objectively. Remember, if you don't ask, you don't get.

Micro-changes, on the other hand, are all about continuing to play in the same places, but making small changes and adjustments to make things easier and increase your chance of winning. Most parents are so busy juggling everything that survival and getting through the week is the only capacity they have. Very rarely has a family had the opportunity to step away from the daily operations to think strategically about how they can win as a family. But when they do, it can make all the difference. For example, instead of stepping back to part-time work to spend more quality time with a struggling child, you could buy back your time by hiring someone to help around the house and prep meals so you can spend the first hour after work playing with your kids. We'll look in depth at buying back your time in Chapter 7. Or you could arrange to start working at 10 am so you can protect time in the morning to invest in your health with a personal trainer.

Regardless of what your winning strategy is, here are a few principles to consider when strategizing how you want to win.

Ritualize what's important: Never leave what is important to chance. If you have big savings goals, set up automated contributions, so your default setting is following through instead of relying on yourself to transfer money every month. If maintaining a strong connection with your spouse is important, sit down and schedule all of your date nights for the next year and make reservations, instead of waiting until the day of to figure everything out. Paddle before the wave, and set yourself up to make it more difficult to cancel your commitment than it is to follow through.

Buy back your time: You can do anything, but not everything. Great families are built by spending large quantities of high-quality time together. Spend the money to delegate tasks so you can expand your own capacity to do what you love. Hire an au pair to live in with your family so they can take care of school pick-ups and drop-offs. Hire a snow removal company so you can snuggle up on the couch with your kids on weekend mornings. Employ your neighbor's kid to cut your lawn so you can take your partner away for a beautiful afternoon at a vineyard. More on this to come in Chapter 7.

Make commitments about how to handle conflict and stress: Conflict is the only way you can build strong and secure relationships. Challenges will be an inevitable part of your pathway to winning. Making commitments as a family about how you are going to handle stress before it happens is a great way to win. For example, make a commitment to "never threaten to leave the relationship" or "always come back together to repair conflict." In Chapter 8, I'll teach you how to use the Family Basecamp to separate facts and emotions and work through issues together as a team.

Making the Call

There are two different leaders out there.

One who is highly attuned to the needs and current state of their family. This leader possesses the ability to be present to the tension of opposing ideas of winning instead of choosing one at the expense of the other, and to build a uniting vision big enough for everyone to win. By doing so, this leader can adapt their family strategy in the short and medium term to support the imminent needs of those they love. They understand that by doing this, they will create a strong foundation to build upon at a later time.

And there is another type of leader, who maintains a strong *pro-self* stance. Instead of creating a definition of winning that is big enough to hold an entire family, this type of leader will get stuck on how the needs and desires of their family members get in the way of them advancing their own personal aspirations, and they will describe their family as an obligation or excuse for why they can't win. Or at times, they are so caught up in their own experience that they overlook the brutal reality and the needs of their dependents and family members, missing out on opportunities to make a difference right now.

After our dinner in Edmonton, Claire realized she had been leading to protect her own interests instead of working with her husband to create conditions where everyone could win. She was committed to changing this, whether she was married or divorced.

About a year later, Claire and I met up again in downtown Toronto over a lunch down by the waterfront. This time, she sat down with a beaming smile on her face. I could tell she was feverishly waiting for the opportunity to bring me up to speed.

As we placed our order and awaited our salads, Claire shared with me that after going through their family strategy, she and her husband had both agreed it was in everyone's best interest that they file for divorce and continue to raise their boys together but separately.

"I can't believe it, Dave. This might sound weird, but even though we are now separated, Andrew and I have never felt closer and more on the same page. The reality is, with two boys together, we are going to be in each other's lives forever. This process not only helped us make the right decision for our family, but it helped us get on the same page for how we were going to win as a separated family. We have a clear vision for the future and a practical understanding of what each of us needs right now. Not only has it allowed us to design a lifestyle that works for us right now, but we both feel confident that as life continues to unfold, we have a great practice to help us adapt along the way. My only regret in all of this is that we didn't do this earlier in our marriage. But it couldn't have happened any other way, because it didn't."

When you take the time to build a strategy for your family, you earn the opportunity to create win-win-win scenarios. It shifts the approach from you versus your family members to you and your family members versus *it*. Life. You can have your cake and eat it too, but it just doesn't happen by chance. You have to strategically design it that way.

Next Play

Strategy creates the container and clarity you need to make decisions. It's time to start defining yours.

1 Guess what it means to win

Defining what it means to win is where it all starts. It creates the container for your family to make decisions, stay aligned, and work together. Take a moment to personally answer the following questions:

1. What does it mean for my family to win right now?

2. What does it mean for my family to win over the next one to three years?

3. What does it mean for my family to win thirty years from now?

Now, it's important to remember that defining what it means to win is a team sport. In order for others to buy into this vision, they must feel included in the process. Take a moment to answer the same question through the lens of your partner and kids. What do you imagine their answer would be? Write down your answers, and then create an opportunity to discuss it as a family to see how accurate you are.

What do you think your partner would say?

1. "What does it mean for our family to win right now?"
2. "What does it mean for our family to win over the next one to three years?"
3. "What does it mean for our family to win thirty years from now?"

2 Remember the future

Bring your family together and create the opportunity to "remember the future." You are going to dream the memories and experiences you would like to create as a family. The insights and interests shared by your family members should inspire your definition of what it means to win as a team.

1. Just imagine you are sitting down together one year from now. What meaningful moments and memories has your family made?
2. Now, fast forward to three years from now. What have you overcome? What are you celebrating? How do you spend your time together?

3. Now travel through time and imagine you are sitting down together twenty-five to thirty years from now. Where does your family live? What magic moments have you experienced together? What stories will you be telling the next generation?

3 Are you playing in the right places?

Choosing where to play will have the single greatest impact on your ability to win, both individually and as a family. Remember, the three areas to focus on are:
1) where you live, 2) where you work/study, and 3) who you spend time with.

1. Where does your family play together?
2. Where is your family spending time and energy, but it is no longer serving you?
3. What pivots does your family need to make to start winning today?
4. Just imagine your family is winning one to two years from now. What has changed?

5

Using Pain as a Tool

A GENTLEMAN NAMED RANDY reached out to me privately after a CEO retreat I ran for MacKay CEO Forums. During our time together, I spoke about how important it is to become a master of conflict repair with your family members. It struck a nerve, and he wanted some help. After I learned about his situation at home, we both agreed the right next step would be to enroll his spouse in the process with him and schedule an initial Couples Coaching call to get on the same page.

After not hearing back from Randy for four weeks, I reached out to check in. "Randy! It's been about four weeks since we last connected. How is your summer going so far? I'm guessing your wife wasn't interested in exploring this work together?"

Randy was silent for a moment. "To be honest, Dave," he finally said, "I haven't even told her about it yet. We've been in a pretty good spot over the last few weeks, so I didn't want to open a can of worms."

Oh, the irony of the situation. Randy had shared that conflict often took days, if not weeks, to resolve with his spouse. Yet, he was avoiding the opportunity to improve their conflict-repair skills while they were in a good spot out of fear that it may be a catalyst to conflict.

What is your relationship with pain?

While pain is relative, everyone experiences pain throughout their life. It shows up in all different forms: physical, emotional, spiritual. The pain can be acute or a chronic challenge we experience for periods throughout life. For some, pain becomes normalized as we learn to live with it day to day.

I broke my back and neck in a hockey accident back in 2006. That type of pain sucks. I hope in your life and in mine that we experience very little of it. But that's not the type of pain I want to focus on here. The pain I'm talking about is the type we experience in relationships with the people who matter the most to us. Resentment. Frustration. Anger. Disappointment.

The goal is that your most important relationships be the harbor you rest in to recuperate and heal. But at times, your family will be a real source of pain. Regardless of how pain shows up in your life, you can rest assured that it will play a part in your story. The question is, how do you respond to it?

Most people have been taught to interpret the sensation of pain as a sign that something is wrong. Over time, we have internalized this narrative that pain is bad. And when we hold this narrative, we naturally do anything to avoid experiencing more pain.

But when it comes to a strong, secure family, everything is built on the foundation of secure relationships. I'm sorry to tell you this, but conflict and hard conversations are the only way to get there. If you avoid conflict, you can't earn connection. But if you embrace conflict and learn how to repair effectively, deeper connection will always be an outcome. Think back to any significant positive change you've experienced in your life. For every single change, a conversation was likely the catalyst for turning your pain into a deeper sense of alignment and connection. To build a strong family, you must start reframing your relationship with pain. Instead of it being something your family avoids, start to see pain as a tool. A tool that, with your leadership, can deepen the way your family works together to win.

So why do we avoid pain so much? There are two primary reasons.

First, past hurt informs future fear. At the core of every human's well-being is an innate need to belong and feel safe. In order to address the pain we experience, we must have a conversation. But we avoid these conversations because we anticipate they might create conflict, tension, disagreement, and ultimately separation and disconnection. Unfortunately, the *real* risk of this happening only compounds over time when we avoid these conversations. Eventually we are sitting on top of a powder keg of resentment from unresolved conflict. Spark a match and *kaboom*.

Second, most of us have no clue what healthy repair looks like. Many of us have grown up watching conflict but have never witnessed healthy reconnection. And since we don't know what it looks like, we don't have the skills to have critical conversations in a way that creates win-win outcomes. To navigate these types of conversations in a healthy way, we need to understand how to be curious enough to deeply understand the experience of the people we love to a level where we can create changes that are in the best interests of everyone involved. When conversations go sideways—because they do—most people don't know how to get things back on track. Instead of deepening trust and safety, conflict compromises it.

Conversations are where change happens and how you reach the next plateau. For a Chief Family Officer, this is the skill that is likely the most under-developed... and the most important. Avoiding pain is how you fall backwards. Think back to the spiral staircase metaphor I shared with you a few chapters back. Conversations are how we move from one step to the next. You can be as clear as day about what it means for your family to win, but if you can't have the conversations to get your family aligned, make pivots, and successfully navigate the changes required to make it happen, all you have is a dream. A dream in the absence of execution is delusional optimism.

So what are some examples of the critical conversations you might be avoiding?

- Conversations with your kids about unhealthy behaviors or decisions they are making

- Unspoken sexual desires
- How your family is spending money
- Issues with extended family members
- Unfair distribution of the tasks of managing the house and kids day to day
- Different opinions of how to support and develop the kids
- Hurt feelings
- Dreaming together about the next stage of your life
- Keeping your family members accountable to the things they are committed to

When we avoid these conversations, a lot of the time we decide to, then do, one of three things:

1 **Leave the relationship:** Unfortunately, when we fail to get what we want, we start to look elsewhere and abandon the relationship. It is very common in parent-child or sibling relationships for conflict and pain to be the reason why they stop talking to one another and go their own ways, often for years, if not a lifetime. In a spousal relationship, this is when we begin dreaming about life with someone else. We may imagine how much easier it would be to live with *so-and-so* because they "just get it." It always breaks my heart to see relationships end because of conversations a couple has been avoiding.

2 **Stall or go backwards:** When we avoid the painful conversation, we begin to accept circumstance as reality. We sacrifice our personal dreams or needs because we perceive the risk of the conversation to be too high. When this happens, we abandon our big hairy audacious dreams and fall into the valley of mediocrity. Funny how we will marinate in stress and the negative energy of contempt and anger for years, but we won't lean into a difficult conversation that could take a day or two and create the conditions for change.

3 **Sabotage and dissociate:** A choice that many make when they can't get what they want is to justify their behavior by blaming someone or something else. This shows up in the form of gaslighting, jealously, criticism, contempt, avoidance, or grudges. By externalizing the issue on the other person, they immediately lose their power to change the situation. Many will dissociate themselves from their circumstance to manage this pain through alcohol, drugs, gambling, diving into more work, or infidelity. Not only does this compromise their ability to reconcile the very issue they are avoiding, but the collateral damage from these addictions and compensatory behaviors destroys businesses and careers.

Many folks avoid these conversations for years, justified under the logic that the other person isn't ready or able to have the conversation. How disempowering. As a Chief Family Officer, it is your job to become a model for your family and learn how to lead these conversations when someone else may not have the same resources as you... yet.

So take a moment and think about a conversation you've been avoiding: something you've been frustrated about, but for whatever reason you have not been ready to have the conversation yet. Write it down in your journal. How long have you been avoiding the conversation for?

Conflict Is the Key Ingredient

Before we talk about how to have these critical conversations, it's important for you to become aware of how you disconnect when you experience pain so you can start to catch it earlier. You can control it, instead of it controlling you.

Throughout our lives, each of us develops a way of reacting when we experience conflict. If you understand your process, it will help you slow down and look closer at the opportunity calling for your attention. This is the first step to learning how to repair faster and more effectively. You will also have a better understanding of the way your loved ones disconnect so that you can become more intentional in the support you offer in those moments. The goal is not necessarily to reduce the amount of conflict you have. All that really leads to is avoidance. Instead, the goal should be to reduce the amount of time it takes to repair and get back on the same page—doing it in a way that brings you back to 101 percent of your connection, not 99 percent.

One of the most meaningful learning experiences I've had was the Couples Coaching program with the Relationship School. While the intention was to expand my coaching skills to be better for my clients, I learned so much about my own conflict-repair dynamics. During this, I learned that there are four different ways we disconnect: avoidance, posturing, collapsing, and seeking.

1 **Avoidance:** When we start to experience tension and pain, many of us disconnect by taking actions to remove ourselves from the situation entirely. This looks like stonewalling others around us and choosing to be non-responsive. It can also mean physically leaving an environment; at an extreme level, avoidance looks like threatening to leave the relationship altogether.

2 **Posturing:** People also react to conflict by digging in their heels, getting loud, and actively fighting for their perspective. Often represented by a porcupine or a puffer fish, posturing is experienced as an aggressive reaction. This quite often leads to others shutting down entirely or making a decision they later regret. A win-lose outcome. If it's hysterical, the pain is typically historical.

3 **Collapsing:** We also react to conflict by choosing to collapse. No, I don't mean physically collapsing on the floor. I mean we unfairly assume full responsibility for the situation and shame ourselves. This response takes an individual completely offline from solving the problem, and it's used to test the relationship and draw the other person in to offer support and soothing. Instead of

solving the *real* issue, leaders often focus on resolving the individual's sadness, fueling co-dependency further.

4 **Seeking:** The fourth way leaders disconnect during conflict is by seeking. I like to describe this behavior as that of the archetypical golden retriever. When you experience conflict, you begin to experience high levels of anxiety that lead you to move closer to the individual. A seeker will often unconsciously create conditions in which they have to connect with the person they are in conflict with, in an attempt to affirm their connection. "Hey, do you know where my wallet is?" "Are you hungry?" "When can we sit down to talk?" "Are you okay to pick up the kids from school tomorrow?" A seeker will disguise their anxiety in the form of seemingly necessary and practical questions. This is a very co-dependent response, and it's rooted in a fear of abandonment or judgment.

My experience has taught me that, depending on the intensity and who the conflict is with, we each have one or two primary ways we disconnect during conflict.

Let Pain Point the Way

Let me share a story about my clients Aaron and Sarah to illustrate how the pain of disconnection can be used as a tool to spot the critical conversations you need to lead your family through to win.

Aaron and Sarah have been married for twenty-five years and raised their two beautiful children (now twenty and eleven years old) on Vancouver Island. For the first ten years of their marriage, Sarah worked retail part-time while taking care of their children and home, and Aaron was running a new custom furniture manufacturing business. At this point in their life, their combined income provided enough to cover their monthly expenses, but as time went on, their lifestyle started to outpace their income. Both Aaron and Sarah were at peace with this, since Aaron's business was due to begin paying significant dividends within the next few years. Their family goal was to build and sell this company so they could enjoy an early retirement.

In 2017, the dividends started to roll in. They were able to pay off their debt and buy a family home in downtown Vancouver. Now feeling more stable, Aaron wanted to start investing in his own personal development. Shortly after his kids returned to school, Aaron discovered a leadership conference for leaders committed to doing good in business and giving back to the world. This was exactly what Aaron was looking for, but it was going to be a significant investment of time and money, as the meetup was coming up quick in December. And took place in Zurich, Switzerland.

Now twenty-plus years into their marriage, Aaron anticipated that Sarah was going to shut down the idea. But Aaron was eager to go to the summit, so he decided to book the trip and purchase a conference ticket without telling Sarah. Instead of creating the space to share with her how important this experience was to him, he avoided the conflict and decided to ask for forgiveness instead of permission. Classic.

And how do you think that went? Not well. As you might expect, when Sarah found out that Aaron was going, she felt that he'd betrayed her and was angry that he would make such a big decision without her. Aaron ended up going to Zurich that year. But because he'd avoided the conversation, not only did the conference cost him a bunch of time and money, but he also lost trust in his most important relationship.

This type of conflict is quite common in any relationship. But there are two ways people deal with these situations. One is to sweep it under the rug and live in the resentment, contempt, and disconnection that come from conflict gone unresolved. The second option is to use pain as a tool. Instead of sweeping it under the rug, create the space to repair after the conflict and develop a deeper understanding of what is *really* going on there.

Yes, Aaron should have asked his wife, or at least enrolled her in the decision-making process. But that is a surface-level issue. Under it is a deeper issue that is critical to their long-term success as a family.

First, Aaron and Sarah don't have a shared understanding of what it means to win. Now that their financial situation has changed so significantly and their children have become more independent, Aaron and Sarah have not come together to build a shared understanding of what it means to win *now*. If they had this understanding and took a proactive approach to their relationship, Aaron would feel supported enough to bring forward these types of experiences without fear of rejection. But this was a new possibility, and Sarah had no idea he was even interested in such a thing.

And second, Aaron and Sarah don't have a predictable way of repairing after they disconnect. Each has their own way of disconnecting: Aaron is an avoider, and Sarah is a posturer. Aaron and Sarah have yet to develop a process for enrolling each other into new opportunities for their family or themselves. Their under-developed communication skills were getting in the way of Aaron feeling comfortable enough to share ideas with Sarah without fear of criticism and judgment, or of Sarah sharing her concerns and feedback without shame or being reminded how much she is like her mother.

When we understand how we and our loved ones disconnect, we can spot the critical conversation and create the opportunity to have it when we are not in the moment and under the stress and pain itself.

Curiosity Fuels Great Conversations

When it comes to critical conversations, most of us make the mistake of trying to understand the situation, come up with a solution, and make decisions all in one single sitting. Critical conversations take time. And they should! There is a lot of insight and understanding that needs to go into the process of building a solution that works for everyone. For you. For them. And for the relationship and family at large.

So instead of trying to get everything done in a single conversation, try seeing yourself as a DJ who is reading the room and stringing together a series of tracks to build a kick-ass set. Only instead of playing music, you're stringing together a series of conversations that builds trust and the courage to make a decision or take an action together.

So how do you approach critical conversations in a way that can deepen your relationship and create an outcome that works for everyone?

When it comes to mastering critical conversations, there is no one better than my friend and mentor Phil Jones, author of *Exactly What to Say*. Phil has taught me that there are three critical ingredients for influential conversations: curiosity, empathy, and courage. Regardless of what your conversation is about, it must always start with curiosity.

Trying to teach someone how to have a critical conversation through a book is like teaching someone how to ride a bicycle through a video game. You may leave with a deeper and better understanding of how, but at the end of the day the only way you will become a strong cyclist is by riding a real bike yourself. And the only way to become better at leading critical conversations with your family is by practicing and doing it in real life. But to start to teach you how, I'd love to share with you a story from my client Martin.

Martin is a manager at a mutual insurance company in rural Ontario and a father to three teenagers: eighteen-year-old Lucie, fifteen-year-old Samantha, and fourteen-year-old Mark. During one of our coaching calls, Martin expressed some of the frustration he's been experiencing with his middle daughter, Samantha. A natural athlete from a young age, Samantha earned a spot on the under-fifteen provincial soccer player development team. Martin and his wife, Carolyn, knew that it would be a big commitment, and they were committed to helping Samantha pursue her dreams of going to an Ivy League school on scholarship. Samantha had a great start, but as the season went on, things started to get tough. Between new demands at school, extra training, and a growing friend group, Samantha began to really struggle with anxiety and depression.

A few days before our call, Martin and his wife were contemplating whether or not Samantha should try out for the provincial team next year. Martin had a pretty straightforward view on the situation. If Samantha wanted to get a scholarship, she would have to start making some significant adjustments to her lifestyle and learn how to better maintain her training and house chores when she was struggling with her mental health. In his mind, this was the cost of doing business and something that Samantha had signed up for.

Carolyn, on the other hand, saw the situation quite differently. Having struggled with anxiety herself, Carolyn could empathize with her daughter's experience and felt that it might be in her best interest to step back from the player development league for a year. In her mind, this would create more capacity for Samantha and their family to stabilize her mental health, transition into high school, and then re-evaluate her commitment to pursuing soccer as a pathway to college or university.

As you might imagine, the different opinions between Carolyn and Martin created some heated conversations. Not to mention the challenge of trying to engage

Samantha in the process. Earlier that week, Martin had tried to bring up the topic with Samantha after dinner one night... but it hadn't gone very well.

I asked Martin, "How did you approach the situation with her?"

"Well, I laid out the situation for her and told her that she needed to make a decision about her future. And that if she wanted to continue to play soccer at this level, she needed to find a way to manage her anxiety and start pulling her weight around the house more, or else her mother and I weren't going to drive her to all of her practices and games anymore. Pressure is a privilege, not a right. Even if you've earned a spot on the team."

"And how did that go?" I asked.

"Not well. As soon as I brought it up, she said that I was overwhelming her and that she didn't want to talk about it. She just went to her bedroom and shut the door."

Most people make the mistake of thinking that it will be helpful if they give context. Martin was trying to get a decision made all in one shot. He thought that by outlining the circumstances and creating a sense of urgency, it would provide clarity and help Samantha.

But the truth is, it does the opposite.

When we try to give context and certainty, it quite often creates uncertainty in the individual we are speaking with. It is our natural inclination to point out why something isn't going to work. When someone tells us how something should be, we naturally conjure up in our minds everything they've missed or don't understand about the situation, especially if it's personal and important to us. And this only creates more disconnection in the relationship. For Samantha, this looked like avoidance. As she avoided the conversation, Martin and Carolyn started to seek more and more—a recipe for a blow-out. This is a great example of a critical conversation approached in the wrong way.

"Martin, if I can ask, do you think Samantha feels understood here?" I asked.

"Dave, I completely understand the situation she is in. She's in grade nine and her whole world is opening up for her. She is making new friends. She is starting to think about her first job. She's inspired by the idea of becoming a professional athlete, but overwhelmed by the amount of work she has to—"

I cut Martin off. "Martin. I didn't ask if *you understand her*. What I asked you was, how certain are you that Samatha *feels understood by you*?"

Processing my question, Martin stared at the ground for a moment. "Uhhh, I'm not sure. Carolyn tells me all the time that Samantha says I don't understand what it's like to deal with anxiety like hers."

"Martin, you must remember, people do things for their reasons. Not yours. You have to find out her reasons. And until you do, the conversation will feel like you and Carolyn are working against Samantha instead of working together to make a decision that is in her best interest. Would you be open to me showing you a different approach you could take here? An approach that will put you and Samantha on the same team?"

Pen in hand, Martin was ready to take down a few notes.

"You see, the person who controls the conversation is the one asking the questions. Listen closely here as I share exactly what to say and ask. First things first, it's important to use your understanding of how Samantha disconnects when she is under stress. Based on the fact that she is an avoider, it is going to be important that she is prepared to enter this conversation on her own, instead of it being sprung on her suddenly. The best way to do this is to ask her a simple question: 'Sam, when would be a good time for us to sit down and talk about your next year of soccer?'"

"I love that!" Martin said. "By asking 'When would be a good time,' I'm assuming that there will be a time, but leaving it up to Sam to choose a time that works best for her. Usually I just bring up this conversation when we are in the car or have a few moments together after dinner while we clean up. I've never really thought about how that might shut her down right away. Okay, what next?"

"It's important to remember the goal of this conversation is not to make a final decision about what to do next year. This doesn't have to happen in one single moment, but instead, see this as a series of conversations that are building toward a decision that is in everyone's best interests. To do this, the goal of your first conversation should be for the three of you to understand how she feels about her experience over the last year and her current thoughts on the year ahead. She should leave this conversation feeling like it makes sense for her to feel the way she does."

A bit confused, Martin stopped me to ask for some clarity. "But what if we don't agree with her, Dave?"

"I'm glad you asked. This has nothing to do with *agreeing* with her perspective, but everything to do with her feeling like you understand it and that it makes sense given everything she's experienced and been through. Remember, you would feel the exact same way as she does if you had all the same collective experiences and DNA as her. And she would see the situation just as you do if she had all of your collective experiences. Until she feels like you understand her perspective and that her view of the situation makes sense, she will not have the capacity to be open to an alternative perspective. At the end of the day, you're looking for Samantha to make a decision about soccer next year."

"Yes, exactly. Carolyn and I spoke earlier today, and we both agree that it's in Samantha's best interest to step down a level next year to get her studies under control, have more time with her friends, and get back to a state of well-being before pushing hard again."

"I love it, but like we talked about earlier, for Samantha to feel good about this decision, it is important that she does it for her reasons, not yours. But here's the trick: most people don't know their reasons for doing anything! Especially kids. So it will help immensely if you can ask the right questions to help her uncover what her reasons might be for making this decision. And the best way to do that is to figure out what's important to her. 'How important is it for you to have time to hang out with your friends after school this year? How important is it for you to win the games that you play? How important is it to play your favorite position? How important is it for you to get a soccer scholarship? How important is it to get a job this year during school?' You see, by asking how important something is, you will help Samantha get clear on her decision-making process and put you and Carolyn in a position to understand her reasons."

"Okay, this makes senses to me, and I can see how different this is compared to my usual approach. But what happens if I find myself wanting to chime in or correct something I don't agree with?"

"It's simple: you stay curious for a little bit longer. One of my favorite questions to ask in these moments is, 'What makes you say that?' This question is brilliant for encouraging the person you're speaking with to continue elaborating on their perspective, while keeping you in a place of genuine curiosity and listening."

About a week later, Martin reached out to let me know that he, Carolyn, and Samantha had had two or three incredible conversations over that weekend. By the end of it all, Samantha had decided to drop down a level of soccer for the next year. Not only was this a big win for Samantha's own well-being, but the conversation ended with a big family hug and a deeper connection instead of a blow-out. By leading this critical conversation with curiosity and creating Samantha's context, Martin brought his family closer together. This experience also helped Martin become much better at asking questions at work.

When it comes to critical conversations, as a Chief Family Officer you have to remember that it's the person asking the questions who leads the conversation. And by asking questions, you can *create* context instead of *giving* context. When you create context and listen until *they* feel understood, you get on the same page as the person you are working with, and you position you and them versus the problem, instead of versus each other. When you do this, you can use pain as a tool to deepen your connection and improve the quality of your relationship instead of breaking them down.

Next Play

Take a moment and think about the way you experience conflict with people in your life.

1 Identify how you disconnect under stress

Write down the names of three to five important people in your life. How do you disconnect when you experience conflict with them? How do they disconnect with you? How long do your conflicts usually last? As a reminder, the disconnector types are avoidance, posturing, collapsing, and seeking.

2 Consider critical conversations

1. What is an example of a time when a lack of curiosity got you in trouble?

2. What do you do right now that makes it difficult for your partner and kids to have conversations with you?

3. What conversations are coming up in your life that could benefit from you being more curious?

4. What would be the most important thing for you to better understand in these conversations?

3 Remember the future

Mastering your conflict-repair skills is critical to becoming a successful leader at home and at work.

1. Describe what it sounds like for you to become a leader who can effectively use pain as a tool.
2. What have you changed?
3. What have you learned?
4. How are you acting differently during moments of disconnection?

6

Protecting Your Most Important Asset: Relationships

BACK IN 2017, my wife Jen and I started to get involved in triathlons and soon found ourselves training for our first Ironman race. This epic swim-bike-run is known as the most challenging single-day sporting event in the world, and the training program to prepare for it is grueling on the best of days.

Up with the birds, my day started with a hot cup of coffee while I packed my bento box with snacks, loaded up my water bottles, and hit the road. Sunday was typically a long-ride day. And on this particular weekend I was embarking on a six-hour-long ride that was bound to push my limits.

When you embark on big challenges like an Ironman, there are some days during training when you feel on top of the world. This was not one of those days.

I wasn't the only one who had plans that Sunday. To squeeze everything in, I'd left at sunrise to get home in good time to help around the house and get the kids ready for their soccer games that afternoon. But as I fought a brutal headwind home, my six-hour ride turned into seven hours of hell. Now about an hour behind schedule, short on food, dehydrated, and miserable, I wheeled into my driveway absolutely wrecked. After putting my bike in the garage and prying my feet out of my biking shoes, I made my way to the front of the house. When you've been riding on a tiny little seat for that long, you don't walk. You waddle. Feeling crunched for time, I had to quickly get some food in my stomach and get the kids ready to leave for soccer, all within twenty minutes. As I opened the door, I saw my middle son, Kalem, sitting on the stairs playing a game on his phone.

"Kalem, what the fuck are you doing, man? Why are you not ready for soccer? What are you doing here wasting time like this?"

Shocked and in silence, tears began pouring down his face as he quickly turned and ran upstairs. I knew right away that I'd messed up big time. The way I reacted in that moment had nothing to do with Kalem and everything to do with me and the state I was in. Your family has a front row seat to all of your experiences. Being this close to the action is good when it's good and hard when it's hard. At this point, I couldn't take back my words. The strength of our relationship before this moment would be the single biggest factor in our ability to repair.

Don't Rehab, Prehab

In sport, rehab is a very common experience for most athletes. On the road to Ironman, pulled muscles, strained joints, exhaustion, and road rash from crashes are par for the course. I remember there were weeks when my knees would swell up with inflammation to a point where I couldn't run anymore. New to the sport, I would typically wait until I was in pain until I reached out to my massage therapist to book an appointment. I can hear Dale, my massage therapist: "David! Why why why do you always wait for your knees to be blown up before you call me? You need to stretch and work on recovering your muscles along the way."

In sport, you can wait to begin the rehab process after the injury happens. Or you can proactively take steps to recover along the way so you can manage the stress that comes from working at such intensity. This is called *prehab*.

To take a prehab approach in sport, you must expect injury will happen. It's a matter not of *if*, but of *when*. When we have this mindset, recovery is no longer a nice-to-have, it's a strategic part of your success and process. In sport, prehab significantly reduces the risk of injury and increases the speed of recovery when it happens. It also allows your body and mind to absorb the training and continue to grow. It involves scheduling massage appointments before you need them. Taking a few moments to stretch after each workout. Or scheduling regular days off to rest and allow your body to absorb the training. An ounce of prevention is worth a pound of cure.

There are many experts out there who can teach you how to do this exceptionally well in the context of sport. Those answers won't be in this book. Instead, I am challenging you to apply the principle of prehab to nurturing and protecting your highest-stake relationships. Much as in sport, the repetitive emotions of day-to-day living will strain and test those relationships. Like I said earlier, the closer the relationship, the greater the vulnerability and exposure to stress, conflict, and challenge. Your mailman won't be affected by you losing a job or coming home exhausted from a difficult bike ride. But your partner and kids sure will be.

When we take a prehab approach to living, we set ourselves up for thirty great years, not just thirty great days. Success is not a thing or an event. It's a feeling you have. A knowing. Especially when it comes to our relationships. We know from great studies like that Harvard Grant Study that people who were most satisfied in their relationships at age fifty are the healthiest at age eighty. And in addition to life satisfaction and physical health, the quality of relationships is highly correlated with an individual's financial success in their peak earning years.

When it comes to building your most important relationships, you have two options. Option one is that you can wait. You can wait for there to be an issue in the relationship before carving out time to identify what's going wrong, and reconnect. Most leaders who choose this option naively believe that their kids will love them forever because they have to. Or since you fell in love, you'll stay in love with your spouse forever. The truth is, most people suck at repairing relationship issues in a healthy and productive way, especially under stress. And strained relationships have a direct impact on our ability to perform and thrive at work. Talk to any leader who has gone through divorce and convince me that their divorce wasn't one of the biggest distractions from their work and personal aspirations.

Option two is that you can create opportunities for carving out quality time on a regular basis before you need to. You expect that your relationships will be tested and stressed. You will forget important events, you will say stupid things you regret, and you will misinterpret the actions of others. If your goal in any relationship is to build lifelong memories together and for your kids and family to want to hang out with you when they have the choice, prehab is a must. When you have strong, secure relationships, this gives you an unfair advantage in business. Because at the end of the day, an incredible person is always community-made.

Not All Relationships Are Equal

Just as you can do anything, but not everything, you can proactively invest in any relationship, but not in every relationship. It's important you understand and intentionally focus on protecting your *highest*-stake relationships.

So what is a high-stake relationship? It is one where the strength and quality of this relationship has a compounding effect on your overall success and well-being. Wealth and health are cool, but what is even more badass is the way people light up when you walk into the room. Or the positive gossiping that takes place when you aren't in the room at all.

There are three layers of high-stake relationships. The first layer, the core, is your spouse or partner. Divorced with kids? Sorry to tell you, but he or she is in there too. The success and well-being of your children is highly dependent on your ability to collaborate. Get the relationship right with your ex, and it will make everything else easier. Get it wrong, and it's like trying to run full speed with a parachute on.

The next layer out is your relationship with your kids and parents. At some point in your life they will both be your dependents, and at other times you will depend on them. Either way, these are high-stake relationships you will have for your entire life.

And the third layer is the family you choose. The best friend you call your sister. The mentor you privately describe as the father you wish you had. The colleague who is your work-spouse; the one who has your back in any fight. The Robin to your Batman.

So, who are your highest-stake relationships? Well, let's look at one of my clients, Garth. Garth is the CEO of an architectural design firm. He recently went through a divorce and is remarried to an amazing woman named Leah. Today they live together as a blended family. Here is a breakdown of Garth's highest-stake relationships from the center out.

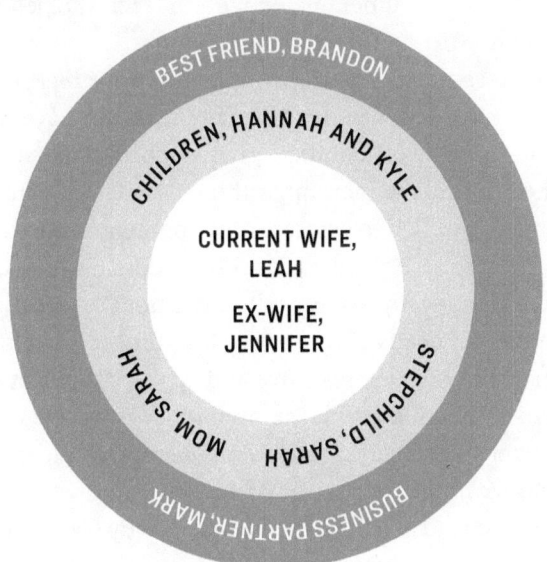

These are the relationships Garth can pull in and lean on when the going gets tough. People like these are also the first people we call when we win to celebrate our accomplishments with. They are also vulnerable to being pushed away. So, who are these people in your life? Go ahead and write in your journal the five to ten relationships that matter most to you.

The Love Bank

When it comes to relationships, unmet emotional needs are the number one reason why couples separate or have extramarital affairs. Prehab is about proactively satiating the emotional needs of the people who matter the most to you and being vulnerable enough to teach the people you love how to do this for you in return. Every one of us possesses the desire to belong. When we feel seen, soothed, safe, supported, and challenged, we have the capacity to navigate conflict, give feedback, and work together to achieve incredible things. As Chief Family Officer, it's your job to create an environment where this can happen for everyone under your leadership.

I don't know any leaders who intentionally overlook the emotional needs of those they love. But instead, the way they naturally express love and appreciation just so happens to not align with the preferences and needs of the person receiving their affection. They haven't learned how to love in the most optimal way yet.

If you've read *The Five Love Languages* by Gary Chapman, this makes sense to you. The classic example is a busy parent buying their kids new toys when all they truly want is quality time playing with the parent and the toys they already have, leaving the kids angry and resentful.

I believe people would do better if they knew better. The trouble is, most people don't know what they don't know when it comes to building strong lifelong relationships.

In business, we lead our teams through assessments and exercises like the DiSC, CliftonStrengths, and Myers-Briggs for a reason. Different folks prefer different strokes. You don't have all the time in the world to invest in relationships, so it is important that you understand how to have the most potent impact. With better awareness we can make better choices. And better choices create better return results and relationships.

When it comes to managing your high-stake relationships, I'd love for you to think about the status of your relationships through the concept of a love bank.

Imagine that you have a love bank for each relationship in your life. With every interaction, you are making either deposits into it or withdrawals from it. Over time, the balance in each relationship will ebb and flow. Your strongest relationships will be in the black. After consistently making deposits over time, we build up savings and a credit. When the going gets tough, we can struggle without risking the relationship. Other relationships float near a balance of zero. In these types of relationships, we make equal amounts of deposits and withdrawals. We can often get by day to day, but the true strength of that relationship is exposed when it experiences stress or conflict. And some relationships will be in the red, which results from making more withdrawals than deposits. This leads to tension, resentment, and stress. Much like with a credit card, you can borrow borrow borrow, but at some point you have to make a minimum payment and clean up your debt. These types of relationships are toxic, demanding, and quietly sabotaging your best energy.

I first learned about the concept of a love bank from Willard Harley. In his book *His Needs, Her Needs*, Willard teaches that every relationship has a love bank, and the balance of this bank is affected by every interaction. Some interactions, like a hug or kiss goodbye, can make small deposits (1 to 5 points). Others will make big deposits, such as spending meaningful quality time together during a shared experience (15 to 25 points). And the same goes for withdrawals. A weird look or saying something the wrong way could make a small withdrawal (-1 to -5 points). Infidelity or lying could drain the account overnight.

There are two ways to influence the balance of your love bank: you can stop making withdrawals from that account, and you can make better and more meaningful deposits.

When it comes to making deposits, it's important to understand that there are generally ten different emotional needs in a relationship: affection, sexual fulfillment, intimate conversation, recreational companionship, honesty and openness, physical attractiveness, financial support, domestic support, family commitment, and admiration. If you are in a monogamous relationship, there will be some emotional needs, such as sexual fulfillment, that only you can offer. Otherwise, most other emotional needs are fair game.

In my relationship with Jen, I have learned that recreational companionship (having fun together doing something we both love), affection, and a commitment to raising great children are her most important emotional needs. Going curling together, playing tennis, snuggling up on the couch together without my phone, and actively celebrating our kids (in addition to the easier task of disciplining) are all ways I can make meaningful deposits in our love bank.

If you are in a monogamous relationship, take a moment to think about your spouse or partner. If you are single, think about the most important relationship in your life right now. In your journal, write their name, the current balance in your love bank (in your opinion), and the top three ways you can make deposits in this relationship.

To put your relationships in the black, you must also learn how you are making withdrawals. This takes a hard look in the mirror. Think about the things you say, the things you do, the reactions and gestures you make when things don't go your way. Withdrawals are anything that makes someone feel overlooked, scared, threatened, anxious, or unwell—pretty much anything that doesn't build emotional needs. And remember, it doesn't have to make sense to you. Someone's perception is their reality. Not yours.

So, what are the top three ways you make withdrawals?

Relationship Overdraft

To help illustrate the principle of a love bank, I'd love to share with you a story from a couple I had the pleasure of supporting.

Married for about twelve years, Alissa and Mark have two beautiful young boys (Luke, five, and Max, two), and live in Texas, just outside of Austin. Mark is an incredibly focused man who is dedicated to his career as a paramedic. His wife, Alissa, stays at home watching the boys and taking care of the house while the boys are at school and daycare. Alissa and Mark are extremely proud of the young men they are raising, but they found themselves in conflict most days, spending their limited time together arguing over logistics. After the boys went to bed, Alissa and Mark would go their own ways, retreating into their respective bedrooms, only to see one another again in the morning as they worked to get everyone out the door for the day. When we first connected, Alissa and Mark described their relationship as roommates raising children together. They reached out asking for help to become a better team and create a relationship dynamic in which they could experience the zest for life and passion for one another that had started their relationship.

As we came to know each other, I could tell that Mark took a lot of pride in his ability to figure things out. The good news was that his interest in and commitment to trying to solve this relationship challenge was there—he just had no idea where to start or what to do differently.

"So, Mark," I opened with, "I'm just curious... what do you believe Alissa's number one complaint about you would be?"

Mark sat back and took a few moments to reflect. "Well, if I had to guess, I would say that Alissa's number one complaint about me is that I don't listen to her perspective or take her opinion, especially when it comes to conflict with my extended family. That is always a sore spot."

As Mark shared his perspective, I watched Alissa move forward to the edge of her seat, barely able to contain her need to comment. "*Exactly!* Honestly, I think I know our neighbors better than I know you, Mark. Every single time we have a problem, you shut down and just tell me that you've 'got it covered.' I'm always on the sidelines and never feel like I know what's going on."

In that moment, I began to witness their conflict-repair cycle... or lack thereof. "So, Alissa, knowing Mark the way you do, why do you think it's so important for him to take care of these issues on his own?"

"Because he's a perfectionist and always wants to be right. But Mark, you aren't the smartest person in this house, you know!"

As the tension started to build, I knew we were making progress. I looked over at Mark and found him staring at his feet. "Hmmm. Mark, is that right? Is that why it's so important for you to take care of issues on your own?"

"No. Not at all, Alissa. I try to take care of the issue on my own because I don't want it to negatively impact you. You do so much for our family all day, so when I come home I often feel guilty and try to solve these problems on my own to avoid putting more of a burden on you. You get worked up and so emotional whenever I share stuff with you."

I quickly jumped in before Alissa could respond. "And how's that working, Mark?"

"Not well. Not well at all, but I don't know what else to do!"

At this point in the conversation, the core issue became crystal clear to me. Both of them wanted a deeper connection but were oblivious to the fact that their current behaviors were making withdrawals from their love bank. While Mark thought he was being helpful by solving conflict and challenges with his family on his own, it left Alissa feeling like her opinions didn't matter. While his being the sole provider for the family took care of Alissa's need for financial support, her needs for openness, honesty, and intimate conversation were being overlooked in the relationship. By slowing down the conversation and getting to the core of the issue, Mark was able to learn that he could still take care of the issue, but do it in a way where he could share his perspective and approach with Alissa along the way.

"So, Alissa, if Mark shared his perspective and approach with you, what impact would that have on you? Why do you think it'd be in his best interest?"

"He wouldn't have to do it alone! We could work together on it and be a team. But truthfully, these arguments almost always happen after we put the kids down for bed. If we worked together as a team on these challenges and Mark opened up, we would fight significantly less and maybe even be in a state of mind where we could start having sex again. Because I'll tell you, when we fight, that's the last thing on my mind. It's been almost nine months since the last time we had sex."

Mark smiled. I could tell the prospect of more intimacy brought joy to him. Sexual fulfillment was likely an emotional need of his that, as with many men, had gone unmet as a result of the disconnection and conflict with Alissa over the last few years. "So, Mark, what are you taking away from this?"

Sitting up straight, Mark admitted, "Well, it's pretty clear to me that what I thought was helping Alissa was actually doing the opposite. I didn't know that Alissa wanted to be a part of the process so much. I just figured she wanted the issue solved."

At this point in time, Mark and Alissa's relationship was in the red. Overdrawn. One of the fastest ways to get out of debt is to take ownership of the role you've played and the impact it has on other people. While Mark realized he had a great opportunity to be more open and intimate with his communication, coming back together wasn't solely on him.

"Alissa," I said, "why do you think it's so difficult for Mark to be open and honest with you when it comes to problem-solving like this?" From the first few moments we met, I could tell that Alissa thought she was doing nothing wrong and that if Mark changed, everything would be different.

After a long pause, Alissa said, "Ahhh, I have to be honest, I don't know. He knows that I want to help, but…"

"But it's not working, Alissa," I said.

Mark reached over and grabbed Alissa's hand. "Alissa, whenever I share my perspective with you, it is inevitably followed by some sort of judgment or criticism about how I am viewing the situation incorrectly. Before I can even share my full idea with you, it feels like I'm already wrong." After being berated for months, this was the first time Mark had the opportunity to share why it was so hard for him.

"So what impact do you think it has on Mark when you judge or criticize his approach?" I asked.

With tears pouring down her face, Alissa said, "He doesn't feel safe to open up to me! My intention is to help, but I guess by jumping in with my own perspective so quickly, it probably makes Mark feel even more protective of my emotions and reluctant to share with me. Wow, Mark, I am so sorry for criticizing you so quickly. I can imagine this makes you feel like shit."

Mark reached out to hug Alissa. While Alissa spoke a big game about wanting more intimate conversation, when she got what she wanted, her critical response and judgment was pushing Mark away instead of pulling him in. By both taking ownership for their respective behaviors, Mark and Alissa were able to repair the resentment building in their relationship. Over time, with this awareness, they learned how to refine the way they work together to make more deposits and less withdrawals going forward, slowly moving from red to black.

As a Chief Family Officer, it is your job to lead your most important relationships. Remember, someone's perception is their reality. You may see yourself experiencing a given situation the same way, but you aren't them. When you learn to care about what the other person cares about, you will build a love bank big enough to do anything together.

Returns Beyond Money

When it comes to making important investments in your life, say your mortgage, do you wait to the last minute every month to flip the couch cushions, clean out the car, and empty your pockets to find loose change in order to make the payment? I sure hope not. You set aside that money as soon as you are paid so that you never default on this payment. Well, if you do this for your house, shouldn't you do this for the most important people in your life?

The truth is, many of us give more quality time to our customers and staff than to our kids and family members. In business, we set one-on-ones, quarterly offsites, or account reviews all the time. Don't you think your children, family, and close friends deserve the same from you too? One of the main reasons we don't do this is because we mistake time spent for *quality* time spent. I get it; busy families spend lots of time together—getting ready in the morning, cooking dinner, doing homework, watching TV, folding laundry, or riding in the car on the way to practices or games. And for some who don't have a lot of time, they assure me that the time they do spend is quality time. But the truth is, strong relationships aren't built from low quantities of high-quality time. They're built from *high quantities* of high-quality time.

So take a moment to think about the parent or child with the lowest balance in your love bank right now. When was the last time you spent more than two hours alone with them, with no electronic distractions, while enjoying a fun activity and quality time together?

When I ask leaders this question, it's often met with a whole bunch of excuses to justify how busy they are. I know life is full. But I can tell you that excuse won't make sense to you when you're lying on your death bed.

So how do you prioritize this time in what is otherwise a time-strapped lifestyle? Create a sense of urgency. Time matters most when it's running out.

As Oliver Burkeman points out, as mortals we generally only have 4,000 weeks to live. If you're reading this book at the age of forty-five, you have approximately 1,660 weeks left to live. Let that sink in. If that doesn't wake you up, think about the number of holiday dinners, vacations, or birthdays you have left to celebrate with your parents. As I write this chapter, my eldest daughter is fifteen years old. That means that I only have three more summers to create a lasting connection with her before she is out on her own. My nana is eighty-nine years old this year. There is a good chance we only have a few more Thanksgiving dinners together.

For some, a lack of urgency seems to be the issue when it comes to creating more quality time together. But for many others, they get caught up in the "how."

While it is important to focus on the day-to-day transactions, I find it extremely helpful to focus on building a system to make regular big deposits. Back in 2022, I met entrepreneur and author Jim Sheils at a global entrepreneurship event I was volunteering at in Palmetto Bluff, South Carolina. As an entrepreneur with five children, Jim is an inspiration to me because of his commitment to building his wealth without sacrificing the strength and connection of his family. I was curious how he managed to make it happen. Jim introduced me to a strategy he used called the Family Board Meeting.

The concept is to carve out three to four uninterrupted hours once a quarter with each of your highest-stake relationships. Once you carve out this time, you go one-on-one with this person, with no electronics, and do a fun activity of their choosing, followed by focused reflection together. In my opinion, the term "family board meeting" implies that everyone is coming together for a single discussion, and it sounds a bit too formal. Instead, I prefer to call this space "strategic solitude." You are strategically carving out time and energy to spend quality time with the people you love in the absence of any distraction or external input.

One of my favorite strategic solitude experiences was going shifter cart racing with my stepson Kalem. Not only did we both get to learn how to drive and race cars (what thirteen-year-old doesn't want to do that!), but it was in that space with no phone or distractions that I could connect with Kalem one on one. Funny how it's always over the cold pop after a fun activity, or on a car ride home, where we really open up and share how we are *really doing*. Some other examples of strategic solitude experiences include bird watching, baking together, going on a biking adventure, or making a big elaborate fort at home.

Much like savings, compound interest matters. This is a strategy that is easy to do, and also easy not to do. Today, in my family, designing our next strategic solitude experience is something our kids can't wait to do. It's something each of us looks forward to every season. Set up recurring times for strategic solitude with each of your highest-stake relationships, and watch your most important relationships flourish. We'll revisit this in Chapter 8 when I introduce you to the Family Basecamp.

Next Play

Take a moment to write down the top three high-stake relationships you want to be more proactive in nurturing. For each individual, reflect on the following:

- What do you believe the current balance is in your love bank?

- How do you unintentionally make withdrawals?

- When was the last time you spent quality one-on-one time together?

- What are some strategic solitude experiences you believe they'd be interested in sharing with you?

Now, take two minutes to take out your phone and send each person a text message to create the space for strategic solitude together. Like this:

"Hey, our relationship is super important to me and I'd like to do a better job of creating opportunities for us to spend more time together. Would you be open to going [insert strategic solitude experience] with me sometime next month?"

7

Designing Your Lived Experience

A FEW SUMMERS AGO I remember coming off the tennis court after a fun afternoon match with a client. While packing up my bag, I bumped into a longtime friend, Meredith, who was catching up on some emails while her kids were stepping on the court for practice.

"Meredith! It's so great to see you! How have you, Steven, and the kids been doing over the last few months? Are they excited for school to be done?"

"Oh man, Dave. I haven't even started thinking about the summer yet. The kids are doing great, but Steven and I are busier than ever. After taking on this new role as vice-president, I've been moving at break-neck speed. Between picking up the kids from school, getting them to their sport commitments, making sure homework gets done, and getting dinner on the table, it feels like the last two years have just evaporated."

"Wow. Life is full for you. I bet you just crash when you hit the pillow at night. And how are you and Steven doing?"

"Steven? Steven who?" Meredith said sarcastically. "Steven is doing great, but we haven't really sat down or spent time together at all over the last few years. Steven has been swamped ever since becoming a partner at his law firm five years ago. We don't have any family in town to help us day to day, so it's been next to impossible to get time together without the kids."

"And are you okay with that?"

"No, but I don't know how we could make it work otherwise. I love making sure that I am always there to take the kids to their commitments, but by the time we do laundry, drive everyone to their sports, fill the fridge with food, and catch up on a few last-minute emails before bed, there just isn't any time in the day for us."

If you talk to any family where there are two working partners with young kids, you'll likely hear a version of this story. And even those with one working parent still struggle immensely to find quality time to spend together.

But the good news is, Meredith is wrong. There is enough time in the day; she just hasn't taken the time to design how she wants to use and leverage her time. And if you have kids, you know that the days are long but the years are short. You have a toddler, and then the next thing you know you are taking your oldest to get their driver's license.

When you don't design how you want to use your time, you fall for the time optimism bias. You believe you will have the time to do everything, yet when it comes down to it, you will spend a fraction of the time, if any at all, on the things that are *really* important. Over time, a gap between vision and reality grows. Many of my clients express how tired they are all the time. Much of this fatigue is a result of spending time doing things that deplete their energy and sense of joy instead of building it through things that really matter to them.

Many leaders make the mistake of trying to get more done with the time they have, but this often only compounds their feelings of exhaustion and burnout. The most impressive leaders I've worked with solve this by taking the time to strategize as a family on how they might *expand* their capacity, a concept that very few have thought about. We've been taught to be mindful of time because it is a non-renewable resource, but what we haven't been taught is how to use our money and creativity to buy back our time and expand our capacity so that we can spend more time doing the things that create value and bring us joy.

Not All Time Is Equal

When it comes to creating more capacity, there are two primary ways of thinking about this. The first is improving your productivity: finding ways to get the things you do done faster in order to get the maximum things done in the minimum time. The second is uncovering opportunities to increase your leverage as a family. And no, I don't mean leveraging yourself with credit. I mean finding ways to get the most things done with the least effort. If you work to improve your productivity and leverage, your capacity as a family can't help but expand.

But before you create more capacity, you must first understand what you are creating more capacity for. What activities do you want to spend more quality time doing? What things are you not getting to?

When it comes to running a business, every job and task is important; however, different values are associated with every activity. In every business, there are administrative tasks like filing paperwork, managing client profiles, and inputting system data. Then there are operational tasks like customer service and coordinating the logistics of programs and services being delivered to clients. And then there are team members responsible for creating new business opportunities and generating the revenue required to fuel the operations. And, of course, there are executive team members who spend their time and energy working on the strategy and positioning the business to win.

The point is, there are different jobs to be done that have different levels of value. This is why roles get paid differently. The greater the value of the task, the more skills required, the greater the paycheck.

A business's ability to continually grow and mature is linked to the leaders' ability to hire great team members so they can spend the most time working on the highest-value items. If not, the capabilities of the team will be underutilized, holding back the company and the leader from their potential. One of the main reasons entrepreneurs struggle to grow their businesses is that they need to make the jump from individual contributor to manager to leader, but they don't know how. Creating space to build systems and hiring key players to lead other activities is how you make this happen. There are people out there who will do those activities significantly better than you, and they'll find joy in the process.

Most of the leaders I work with are incredible at doing this in business, but they really suck at doing it at home.

So let's start to figure out what are the most important activities at home that create value for your family and give you energy.

Design Your Role

To help you get clear on this concept, I am going to use one of my clients, Lisa, to illustrate how to get started.

Lisa is forty-seven years old and works as a VP of operations for a large Canadian bank. Newly divorced, Lisa has full-time custody of her children. Now ten and seven years old, her kiddos are busier than ever with school, sports, and friends. Over the last three years, Lisa has become devoted to her yoga practice and is actively learning to become a professional coach, with ambitions to run her own business in the next five years—all while also trying to start dating again and creating the space to meet a new partner to enjoy life with. During one of our coaching sessions, Lisa expressed how little time she had to work on her coaching business. She knew in her heart that building this business would be a vehicle for creating more freedom and wealth for her family. Lisa's definition of winning as a family was to move to Costa Rica for the winter every year and travel the world together while learning and working abroad. With so much on the go, she had very little time for the work that would get her there.

In every home and business, there is a series of "jobs to be done." Things that just have to happen so we make the progress we seek or live up to the commitments we've made. But our commitments almost always outpace our capacity. You've heard me say it before, and I'll say it again: you can do anything, but not everything.

In Lisa's case, finding an extra fifteen minutes here or there is not going to make a difference in her life at work or home. At some point, productivity has limited upside. Many of my clients have tried absolutely everything they can to become more productive and are still falling short. Leverage is the greatest opportunity for Lisa.

But before buying back your time and finding leverage, you have to understand what "jobs to be done" you will be doing yourself, and what jobs you need to fire yourself from or replace with someone or something else.

With Lisa, we pulled up her calendar from the week before and walked through a week in her life to capture all the things she is and is not doing—the planned work and the unplanned stuff that pops up.

"So, Lisa, now that we've walked through a week in your life, let's talk about how you are spending your time right now. You know that in business there are different jobs that have different value associated with them. Some jobs create tons of value, some very little value, and lots in between.

"In your journal, divide your paper into four sections: $$$$, $$$, $$, and $. What I'd like you to do is take five to ten minutes to review last week, write down all the tasks and jobs you do throughout the week, and organize them based on the value you feel they create for you and your family."

Without hesitation, Lisa started making a list in her journal. She turned it for me to see once she was done.

$$$$—Highest Value
- Disciplining and supporting the kids during tough times
- Taking the kids on adventures and new experiences
- Training to become a coach and business owner
- Researching homes/schools/community in Costa Rica
- Supporting aging parents

$$$
- Helping the kids with homework
- Communicating with teachers/doctors, etc., to support the kids
- Taking care of my own health (yoga, etc.)
- Working on family finances and budget
- Having fun with my friends/going on dates
- Planning for kids' camps/extracurriculars
- Bedtime routine

$$
- Making the kids healthy meals
- Grocery shopping
- Driving the kids to sports/friends/school
- Working around the house
- Coordinating child care
- Holiday gifts and celebrations

$—Lowest Value
- Cleaning the house and dishes
- Laundry
- Walking the dog
- Taking out the garbage
- Cutting the lawn/landscaping
- Changing water/air filters at home

"This looks great. So who is doing all of this work now?" I asked.

Lisa laughed. "Uhhh, me, myself, and I."

"Okay, so let's imagine we are going to design your life and how you spend your time and energy every day. Without worrying about how everything else will get done, write down a list of the jobs you would like to dedicate your time, energy, and focus to. The jobs that are important to you and bring you joy."

"That bring me joy?" Lisa asked.

"Well," I said, "just because an activity or job is low in value doesn't mean you should be stepping away from it.

Some people absolutely *love* cleaning. While they could easily hire someone to do the work for them, it would take away the opportunity for them to enjoy a couple hours of puttering around the house and the stress relief that comes from cleaning everything up. Others may want to quietly puke at the idea of cleaning. It's all about building a job for yourself that not only creates the most value but also brings you joy in the process!"

After a few minutes, Lisa spun around her notebook again for us to review her list together.

"Okay, so now that we've gotten clear on what you *want* to spend your time and energy on," I said, "let's make a list of the jobs you want to fire yourself from."

As she sat back taking a deep breath, I could tell Lisa was starting to imagine how her relationship with her kids would change if she was able to fire herself from many of the tasks that were quietly sabotaging her time and energy.

"All right," she said, turning the notebook back toward me again, "here you go. Making meals. Grocery shopping. Landscape work around the house. Changing water and air filters. Taking out the garbage. Laundry. Cleaning the house. This is all the shit I hate doing but just has to be done."

"Okay, great. What jobs would you fire yourself from first?" I asked. "What is getting in the way of you being able to go on bike rides with the boys, getting to bed in good time, or having the time to find a family therapist? What's the stuff that frustrates you?"

Lisa laughed out loud. "Ha! Laundry, laundry, laundry. I swear, between school, playing outside, and sports, those boys have a never-ending pile of dirty clothes. Once I finally get them down for bed, I am right into the living room folding laundry and making lunches for the next day. I'll be honest, at that point I am so gassed that I end up pouring myself a glass or two of wine and throwing on a couple Netflix shows. Now that I say it, the shows and wine every night probably aren't helping my sleep at all. Other than that, I think cooking meals is the other big one."

I nodded. "Brilliant. I'm curious: How many hours a week would you say you spend on laundry and cooking?"

Scribbling in her notebook, Lisa did some quick math. "My guess is fifteen hours a week."

"Okay, and just imagine we could give you back fifteen hours every week and find another way to take care of all the laundry. How would that impact your new business and your goal of moving to Costa Rica for extended periods of time?"

"Wow, uhhh, I've never ever thought of that as a possibility. At this rate, it will likely take me three years or so to become a professional coach and have my own practice. I just don't have the time to do program or business development. So on the work front, if I could get fifteen hours back a week, I would be able to exit my current role and become self-employed within twelve to eighteen months. And as for my health and relationships with the kids? Shit, it'd be incredible to have that time back. Spending quality time with the boys is the most important thing for me, and I know they absolutely love our bike adventures down the creek together. I'd be able to spend time finding not just any therapist, but the right support for my boys. I mean, if I could go to bed on time instead of staying up late doing laundry most nights, I would... well, I don't even know the impact that would have, because I can't remember what it feels like to have a full night's sleep since having the boys. Okay, I get it, but how do I do this, Dave? Or is this just a dream?"

As her excitement continued to build, I sat back and smiled.

Trade Money for Time

When it comes to managing money, most people only think about trading either time for money or money for money.

We trade our time for money at work every day. We put in thirty-five to forty or more hours of work each week and take home a salary or paycheck for it. While you may be on salary, you are fundamentally trading your time and energy to earn a living and generate active income.

And once we start to amass savings, we earn the opportunity to trade money for money. We invest our hard-earned savings into the stock market or investment properties or leverage high-interest savings accounts to allow our money to work for us. We use our money to create more money. This is passive income.

Yet, most people and families overlook a third type of trade: trading our money to buy back our time. Trades such as valet parking, snow removal, and house cleaning. This is where you have the opportunity to create real leverage and expand your capacity as a family. Capacity to not only spend time doing more of what you love, but also spend time doing things you've never had the capacity for before.

The reality is, we are each replaceable. Every job we do, someone else can do equally well, if not even better than ourselves. Every single day, we make a choice to hire certain people, services, or products to do various jobs for us. This morning your kids likely "hired" you to make them breakfast. Every night you "hire" your bed to help you recover and become well-rested for the day ahead. When you go grocery shopping, you are hiring the market to provide you with fresh food.

And when you are no longer satisfied with the way a job is being done, you will fire someone or something and hire someone or something else. When your car breaks down, you will fire old Betty Blue and buy a new car. While you wait for the new car to arrive, you may hire an Uber to get you from A to B. If your doctor or teacher is no longer supporting you in a meaningful way, you may look to hire another medical professional or educator to help.

At the time Lisa and I were working together, she was hiring herself to do everything—a common story for single parents, or any family for that matter, especially if you grew up in a family where self-achieved independence was celebrated and you watched your parents take pride in doing everything on their own. But if Lisa wanted to spend more time on the activities that were going to help her family win, she needed to buy back some of her time.

"Lisa, if you want to win as a family, you need to fire yourself from a few jobs," I said. "So right now, you hire yourself to do the laundry. What are four or five alternative ways to get this job done?"

"I guess I could hire a full-time nanny to manage our house and make sure our laundry is done. I could ask my mom to come by once a week to do the laundry now that she is retired and has some extra time. Or, now that I think of it, I could use one of the local laundromat wash, dry, and fold services. I think there is actually one that would come right to my house to pick up the laundry on the doorstep!"

"Excellent. Now what's your buy-back rate?" I asked.

With a confused look on her face, Lisa asked, "My buy-back rate? What do you mean?"

"Based on your income, how much money can you afford to spend on buying back your time to focus on higher-value activities with your work and family?"

"Uhhh... I have no idea. How do I know that?"

"Simple. Take out your calculator, type in the total gross annual income for your home, and divide by 8,000."

Lisa quickly pulled out her iPhone and worked out $175,000 divided by 8,000. She turned her phone for me to see the final calculation: "$21.88 per hour!"

"Wicked, so now you know what you're working with. This isn't a bulletproof number by any means, but it is very helpful for understanding the rate at which you can afford to buy back your time. This will help you narrow down the options for hiring someone else to get the jobs done that are in the way of you living a life more full of the things that bring you joy."

"Wait wait wait. Help me understand the math," Lisa demanded.

"It's not a perfect equation, but the goal is to get an estimate of what you can afford. Most leaders work, on average, 2,000 hours a year. So if you divide your annual salary by 2,000, you will arrive at your approximate hourly wage. In your case, this would be $87.50. If you were to use your hourly wage as your buy-back rate, it would be too high for you to feel comfortable trading your money to buy back your time. So instead, aim for about 25 percent of your hourly wage as a good starting spot for what you can afford, while understanding that in many cases the hours you buy back can be used to earn more income. In your case, the hours you buy back can be used to spend quality time with your kids and accelerate your ability to earn more through your coaching business. So, by dividing your annual salary by 8,000, we just eliminate a step in the process to get to your final number a bit quicker. Dan Martell taught me this!"

"Okay, awesome," Lisa said, "that makes complete sense, and wow… this is fun now, having an idea of what type of money I can spend to hire some help."

"So let's go back to the options you came up with to outsource your laundry," I suggested.

With enthusiasm Lisa jumped right into it. "Awesome. Well, now that I think of it, while my mom could help, I don't really want to mix family and work like that. I want my mom to have time with her grandchildren and me without any weird feeling that she is expected to work while she is here. Hiring a nanny might work in the long run, but I think it's overkill right now, and it would be quite a bit of work to find someone who would be a great fit. But the laundromat service could work great, except I just don't want them to fuck up our clothes or dry things that should be hanged. Know what I mean?"

"I sure do. It's really important that you think about this as an experiment when hiring something new to buy back your time. A way I like to think about this is 'one—three—many.' Try out the service for one week and see how it goes. Use that experience to make some adjustments, and then try it out for another three weeks. After that, you will have enough experience to decide whether to continue to use this service for many weeks to come. Or you can decide to stop and look for another option if it doesn't work out. But the most important thing is that you decide to experiment and challenge your assumptions about what might go wrong."

"I love this! I spend about five hours a week doing laundry at home, so if I can use this service for $100 a week, it would be worth it. Shit, I might even start looking for someone to help me prepare lunches and dinners a few times a week, now that I know my buy-back rate."

Right after our time together, Lisa signed up for a local laundry service. When we connected during our coaching session the following month, Lisa jumped on with a huge smile on her face.

"Dave, why the hell didn't I do this earlier? I didn't realize I was hiring myself to do so much, and how all of those small jobs were, yes, important, but getting in the way of me doing so much more. This laundry service is incredible. For the first time in years I am now going to bed when the boys do. I can spend extra time snuggling with them before lights out, and when I have the energy, I have time to work on my coaching program and browse some online dating profiles. I have my first date next week!"

Live a Life You Love

At the end of the day, strategically looking for opportunities to buy back your time is all about empowering yourself to live a life you love. A life that fuels you, gives you energy, and affords you the opportunity to invest your time and attention in the things that matter to you. One that inspires your kids and community to do the same.

Just like Lisa, once you start to experience the life-changing effect of expanding your capacity, you will never play the game of life the same. Depending on your context and circumstance, the way you expand your capacity may even be just a short-term strategy to get through a particular season of life.

And there are simple and small ways to do this job by job. More than ever we have access to an abundance of services to simplify our life and save time. Instead of going to the grocery store each week, you can now use an app or online service to pick up and deliver your grocery orders. If you are trying to eat more consistently but struggle to find the time to cook healthy, calorie-conscious meals, you can easily find a local cooking service to prepare and deliver meals to your family. Or you can hire cleaners to come into your home once a week to do the deep clean you vehemently avoid. If you've been overlooking these opportunities to buy back your time, start here.

As you start to experience the value of this work, there will come a time when you have the opportunity to commit to a longer-term strategy, one that simplifies how you take care of all the jobs you don't want to do.

A great example of this is my dear friend Mike Brown. Mike and I met in Boulder, Colorado, back in 2017 in the living room of our mutual coach and friend, Philip McKernan. After retiring from the military as a fighter jet pilot, Mike had started and sold a business in the oil and gas sector and was in the early stages of starting a new coaching business: Unbreakable Wealth. At the same time, Mike was in the process of going through separation and divorce with his first wife.

One of the things that impressed me most about Mike was not how good an entrepreneur he was or how intentional he was in his effort to be an incredible father, but his ability to continually create space for himself to experience adventure and awe. Whether it was mountain bike races, plant medicine retreats, or heli-skiing with his buddies in the Colorado Rockies, Mike seemed to have found a way to make it all happen. But what surprised me most was his ability to be deeply present. For a single parent with so much on the go, I would have expected

Mike to always be on his phone trying to manage everything from afar, yet he was present and undistracted. So one day while driving through the mountains together, I asked him, "Mike, how do you do it all?"

Chuckling while taking a sip of his coffee, Mike responded, "What do you mean, Dave?"

"Well, I have two kids myself and run a business. Coming out here takes a lot of work. I mean, it felt like I had to move mountains and build a whole team to take care of our kids while I made the trip to Colorado this weekend. Yet, you seem to be bouncing around doing exciting stuff multiple times per month without batting an eye or being completely overwhelmed with managing everything from your phone. How do you do it?"

Without hesitation, Mike responded, "Oh! I have a house manager, dude. Didn't I tell you?"

"A house manager? What the hell is that? I didn't know you still lived at home with your parents," I said jokingly.

For the remainder of our drive, Mike explained to me how he hired someone part-time to help him take care of his house and the day-to-day operations of his family so that he could continue to live life on his terms, even as a single parent.

Intrigued by the concept and eager to learn more, I asked, "So, what exactly does your house manager do? How much do you pay him or her?"

"Oh man, April is absolutely incredible. The mornings around our house are an absolute zoo. After I get up with the kids, we have some breakfast and then I get them off to school on the way to work. Once we leave, April swings by and does a quick ten-minute tidy to make sure the house is all clean and reset for when we return home at the end of the day. And we've built a bit of a weekly routine. On Mondays, April always hits up the local market to fill our fridge with food for the week. She knows the staples we like to keep on hand at all times, and then I just text her a small list of the extra food we need for the week ahead depending on who is coming over and what our plans are. On Wednesdays, April does all of our laundry and turns over the bedding and towels throughout the house to make sure things are fresh and ready to go. And then at the end of each day, April swings by the kids' school to pick them up so I can work until 4:30 or 5 each day without having to leave mid-afternoon to do the hour-long pick-up loop. April works with us about twenty to twenty-five hours a week, and we pay her $25 an hour. Other than the usual routine each week of doing laundry, buying groceries, watering the gardens, and maintaining a clean house, she is always available to help me run one-off errands and schedule appointments for myself, the kids, or anything we need done at the house. It's been a game changer. But that's my secret!"

Can you imagine how your life would be different if you had an extra pair of hands to help get things done for your family each and every week, almost like a personal assistant? This was Mike's secret for being able to lead a life he loves, show up fully as a parent, and do it all without living in a state of constant stress and exhaustion.

You Can Have Your Cake and Eat It Too

After learning this from Mike, I started to realize he wasn't the only leader I knew who was leveraging this strategy. There were dozens of people in my community, like Jessica Woodbeck, CEO of Thrive Realty, who has a full-time life manager employed under her company to help her family thrive as she works to build one of America's top boutique brokerages.

I was inspired, but this remained just a "good idea" until we had our third child, William. When we found out we were expecting him, Jen and I were a bit shocked and unsure of how we would continue to make everything work as a family. Most importantly, how would we continue to run our businesses, show up for our big kids (who at the time were ten and twelve years old), have the time and energy to move our bodies every day, play the sports we love, and travel, and continue to protect the time and space to invest in our own relationship? We just couldn't see it all working. Our commitments were greater than our capacity. We knew that if we wanted to have it all, if we wanted to play to win, we would have to expand our capacity. That was the only way.

For some families like Mike's, a part-time house manager works great for dealing with a handful of recurring activities that would lighten the load. In many situations, you can easily find someone you trust in your community who is looking to earn some more money. A win-win. Many hands make light work.

But for us, given the unique dynamic of our busy family, we needed more day-to-day support to help with the unplanned work and last-minute changes. When we sat back to talk about the right type of help, we immediately gravitated toward a full-time live-in nanny. But after looking into the process of recruiting a nanny internationally, applying for the visa, and getting them on the payroll, we realized the cost of this approach was more than our family could afford at the time.

It was during this process that we discovered the au pair model. Unlike a full-time live-in nanny, an au pair is typically a young adult from another country who helps with housework or child care in exchange for room, board, a bit of cash, and, most importantly, the opportunity to learn and practice a new language.

When we sat down to evaluate the potential of this opportunity, it checked all the boxes. Unlike the full-time live-in nanny, the au pair program cost us only $1,000 per month and fit right within our buy-back rate and family budget. And it didn't require a long and complicated visa process. For us, this was a great experiment worth exploring.

And wow, did it work well and exceed our expectations in so many ways. At the time of writing this book, we have had a total of four au pairs come to live with our family on six-month terms. Jen and I would both say that it is the secret to our thriving marriage and a big reason why we have the capacity we do to run our businesses and do the things we love, both individually and as a family. I think back to the day Jen put the Post-it note on our fridge during one of our most difficult seasons. I'm not sure what our relationship and businesses would look like today if we were still doing everything ourselves.

Over the last three years of working with au pairs, the biggest surprise to me has been the reaction from our community. Of course, as I was with Mike, many people are curious about how it works. But I was most surprised by the negative reactions some folks had: "I would never want someone else to raise my children." "My parents would die if they knew I had help like that." "I could never trust someone to live in my house with me."

You see, I don't take this personally. People's reactions merely reveal the limiting beliefs many parents have when it comes to how they run their family. Even when a solution stares us right in the face, we are often overwhelmed by fear of judgment, so we fail to explore and experiment to see how it might work and if our assumptions are even true to begin with.

A common misunderstanding is that we use au pairs to parent our children exclusively so we can galivant around the world and selfishly do what we want, leaving the raising of our children to someone else. That is just not true. We have designed the job for our au pairs so that we can significantly increase the amount of quality time we can spend with our kids when we are with them. Instead of folding laundry or tidying up the house for the tenth time that week, we can come home and jump in the pool to play with the kids for an hour before dinner. Or we have the time and energy to support our kiddos on a challenging issue with their friends, rather than having to think about "what's for dinner" while trying to hold space for the ones we love the most.

The top two reasons leaders fail to give themselves the opportunity to experiment with a solution like this are 1) their unconscious fear of judgment, and 2) their worry that someone else can't get a job done to their standard or liking. Just imagine you found a way to fire yourself. What would be your biggest worry?

As you begin to explore opportunities to buy back your time, you must remember one very important thing: your family is not your parents' family. When you got married, they did not get another son or daughter in their family—you started your own family. So make decisions to build your family by *your* design, not theirs. Because your family wants the best of you, not what is left of you.

Next Play

Let's start buying back your time.

1 Use joy as your GPS

First, write your ideal job descriptions: the jobs that need to be done that bring you joy. Have your partner do the same. Make sure you include the things you haven't had the capacity to get to.

Take a moment to review your lists together. How can you shift the way you get things done within your family to create more joy for everyone?

2 Make an outsourcing plan

If you could engage someone to help with your family, what is the job description you would write for them? What jobs to be done would you assign to them? Without figuring out *how* or *who* it is, start by writing down *what* you would dream of having someone else do. What are the first two or three jobs you would gladly outsource?

What impact would it have on your career, your health, and your relationships if you were able to hire someone to help you with these jobs?

3 Identify the unseen obstacles

What are you worried about? Depending on how you grew up, this approach to living may be quite new to you. That means there is a good chance you are going to have some anxiety about a few things. Name them.

4 Run an experiment

Now that you have a job description and a breakdown of all the things you'd like to fire yourselves from doing, you're ready to start building an experiment. Set a timer for ten minutes and each come up with three different small bets you could place to experiment with buying back your time. Decide on one experiment and give it a shot.

8

Staying Connected and Aligned

HER FEET SOAKED IN a mixture of blood and mud, Jessica and her team were approximately a mile out from their next checkpoint. Now that they were three days into a week-long adventure race across the Appalachian Mountains, the grueling days were settling in.

An Ironman champion, Jessica Kuepfer had mastered transitions and checkpoints for single-day races. For an independent athlete, aid stations were merely a signpost for progress, an opportunity to take a quick pee or reload on fuel for the miles ahead. There was nothing to them.

But this race was different. Now she was on a team of five athletes. Jessica and her team were responsible for navigating their way across 275 miles of unmarked forest, carrying their own food and supplies, all while mountain biking, hiking, and canoeing. Over the course of the week, each team was due to reach seven checkpoints to complete the race—approximately one each day. Jessica's team always called these checkpoints their basecamp.

Jessica's team captain, Bradley, built a race strategy to win. This unfortunately meant the team was going to race through the first two evenings with little to no sleep. She explained to me how it worked:

The reality is, with five team members, we each have to manage our own energy, injuries, mental struggles, and fatigue along the way. Basecamps are mission critical to our team's success. Of course, we use this as an opportunity to sit down for a moment and have a bite to eat, but the real magic is in the discussion. During basecamp, we always discuss where we have been, where we are at, and where we are going.

When we talk about where we've been, this gives us an opportunity as a team to reflect on and celebrate the exciting and challenging moments from the stage we've just completed. This is where we get to express our frustrations, give gratitude, and let things go. We give ourselves the opportunity to absorb all the work we've done and acclimatize to our new stage.

Then, our team captain always does a pulse check on where everyone is individually. As a team we talk about two important things: Where are we playing from a place of strength right now, and where are we feeling nervous, anxious, or weak? Since we always race to win, it's critical that our team captain understands how we are really doing. And of course, it's incumbent on team members to put their egos aside and be honest. This allows us to make big decisions about food, sleep, and team assignments. With more awareness, he can make better choices that reflect our team capacity. Sometimes we have extra energy to push a bit harder, and other times we are hanging on by a thread.

And of course, then we talk about where we are going next. The next leg of the journey. This keeps us focused on what is coming up and helps us get clear on our approach. After our check-in, Bradley will often assign roles to various team members to distribute responsibility so he can continue to focus on the big picture. For example, Bradley will sometimes assign a "mother" role to select team members, bestowing the responsibility to monitor the well-being and nourishment of all team members during the next leg. Or when some team members are struggling to carry their weight, Bradley will bestow a "mule" role on team members who have the capacity to carry extra weight.

We see a lot of teams in the adventure racing community spend all their time training for the actual sports, overlooking arguably the most important aspect of team sport: communication. Our basecamp is something we practice on a regular basis. It's a huge part of our race strategy and, if you ask me, one of the main reasons we win so regularly.

Whether you're doing multi-day adventure racing, scaling some of the world's most challenging mountains, operating a small-to-medium enterprise, leading a Fortune 500 corporation, or raising a family, staying aligned with and attuned to your team is critical. If you get it right, your team will thrive together, and if you get it wrong, you will have a front row seat when your ambitions fall into the rearview mirror. A good coach builds a gameplan. A great coach changes and adapts his or her plan based on new information.

When your family is working well together, it can feel like anything is possible. And when things aren't going well, it can feel like death by a thousand cuts. You are only as good as your least well family member. By now, you've gotten clear on what it means for your family to win. This is family leadership. But just because you're clear on where you want to go doesn't mean your family will get there by default. Family management is where the rubber meets the road.

In long-distance races, it's the pebble in your shoe or the odd stitch in your shirt that seems insignificant at first but over time becomes all-consuming, the root cause of the agony you feel step by step. For many, this is the reason they quit. The same is true for your high-stake relationships. While significant blow-outs can happen, simple miscommunications are what often create points of irritation in a relationship and a family. Like a blister, they start small, but over time they can become the central point of focus. Most relational issues come down to unmet expectations.

"Hurt, disappointment, and frustration result when there is a wide gap between what we expect and what actually happens," says family therapist Mitch Temple in his book *The Marriage Turnaround*. "The closer we can get our expectations to line up with the truth, the less hurt we will experience."

So how do you stay on track? How do you adapt to unexpected challenges and exciting new opportunities that you come across along the way?

By adopting a basecamp mentality.

Instead of waiting for a surface-level issue to grow into resentment, a basecamp mentality is all about proactively creating the space to reflect and continuously recalibrate expectations along the way. The time and energy you invest here is another form of prehab for your most important relationships. As the Chief Family Officer, you must lead this process and create the conditions that bring everyone together. But an adventure race has a start and finish line. Leading a family is like climbing a peak-less mountain. There is no end, just a series of new beginnings and thresholds to cross.

To adopt a basecamp mentality, you must acknowledge that all teams and families are made up of imperfect people. Yes, you too. I know it's hard to believe. And not only imperfect people, but an imperfect plan that will need adjustments along the way.

If there were one thing you could do as a family that would make everything else significantly easier, it would be coming together for two critical conversations:

1. The Family Basecamp
2. The Weekly Reset

Both the Family Basecamp and the Weekly Reset are a series of short, intentional, and predictable check-ins with your entire family to get on the same page and talk about how you can best support one another to win. The Family Basecamp happens four times a year, and the Weekly Reset happens—as you may have guessed—every week.

The Family Basecamp

In anticipation of the New Year, most families and businesses routinely create space in December to celebrate the year that passed and begin to construct New Year's resolutions, goals, and plans for the year ahead. This is no doubt a helpful and fun exercise, but as Brian Moran and Michael Lennington remind us in *The 12 Week Year*, when we operate off annualized thinking, we mistakenly believe there is a lot of time left to get things done.

And, Brian Moran illustrates, we act accordingly. "It happens all the time in the insurance and financial services industries. For many agents and firms, December is traditionally the best month of the year, and the fourth quarter often represents 30 to 40 percent of the annual sales. It is amazing what happens when people have a goal and a deadline."

I bet you're a bit like me: December comes around and you get all excited about the year ahead, setting goals to spend more one-on-one time with your kids, get in shape, or take on a new personal challenge such as learning a new language. Before you know it, March rolls around and you haven't done any of the above but remain hopeful that it will happen sometime in the year ahead. But it never does.

If there is one game-changing practice for a family, it's the Family Basecamp. Instead of an annualized approach to your family planning, it empowers your family to work from the far more powerful mindset of the twelve-week year. When you operate off a twelve-week year, you can adapt how your family runs to stay attuned to what's most important.

When it comes to planning, you will have a much clearer vision when you look ahead twelve weeks instead of twelve months. The Family Basecamp forces your family to get clear on what's most important while remaining highly attuned to the needs and challenges of each member. By coming together as a family every three months, you are creating four times the number of opportunities to celebrate the accomplishments you've made as a family, while leveraging the innate excitement and anticipation that comes from a new beginning. The Family Basecamp will empower you to build your family by design, one quarter at a time.

You might be wondering, "What do I cover during the Family Basecamp?" "How much time do we need?" "Should we include the kids?" "How do we capture everything we discuss?" Here is our playbook for the Family Basecamp.

Where

The Family Basecamp should be something your family members look forward to. That means that where you do it matters. The place you select to host your Family Basecamp should be inviting, comfortable, and free from potential distractions. Each Family Basecamp takes approximately three hours to complete together as a family. Some of our clients' favorite locations include the family cottage, a picnic in the backyard, a favorite hotel room, a big table at a local restaurant, or a table at a local park.

Most importantly, the environment should be comfortable and a place everyone enjoys spending time in.

Who

Every family member should be welcome to attend and contribute to the Family Basecamp. That said, if you have children, you know that at times kids, depending on their age, can be more of a distraction than anything. The primary purpose of this exercise is to create a twelve-week gameplan so your family can experience more connection and intentional living throughout the year. If you can create connections during this time, that's great. But the main focus is to come out with a gameplan.

If you have children under the age of seven, I recommend you secure child care so you can have three to four hours of uninterrupted time between you and your spouse. You can always share some of the highlights with your children afterwards, such as what you're looking forward to, but this will allow you the attention you need to get the work done.

If you have children aged seven or older, I recommend you actively engage them in this process. Not only are their contributions important throughout, but also each Family Basecamp creates a real opportunity for you to demonstrate to your children what it looks like to build a life by design, so they can learn from what you do. By including them in this process, you are not only creating the conditions for your family to flourish together, but you are also equipping them with the skills to do this with their own family one day.

What

Okay, now let's talk about what to cover. Ideally, your family should be working through the same questions at every Family Basecamp. Here is a list of the most important topics to cover during your time together:

Rose—Bud—Thorn
Ask each family member to share the following:

- **Rose:** Something great that happened over the last ninety days
- **Bud:** Something they are looking forward to in the next ninety days
- **Thorn:** Something they struggled with over the last ninety days

Family Member Check-In
- How is their mental and physical health?
- How is school or work going?
- How are their relationships?
- Where are they winning right now?
- Where is each family member feeling nervous, anxious, or weak?

Schedule Your Family Life Before Your Work Meetings
- What are the two or three most important things for each family member over the next ninety days?
- What are the important dates coming up this quarter?

- How is your family going to be spending quality time together? When is this taking place?
- How is everyone investing in their health? What time and space are required for this?
- When are you and your partner going to be spending one-on-one time with each other? With the kids?
- Is there any travel in your calendar? Who is going where, when?

Looking Around the Corner
- What important events or experiences are coming up over the next twelve months?
- What can you do over the next ninety days to proactively prepare for these?

Critical Conversations
- What are the primary issues you are trying to solve right now?
- What conversations does your family need to be having over the next ninety days?
- What conversations have you been avoiding?

Who's Leading What
- Take a moment to discuss your family's key activities for the next ninety days.
- Decide who will be responsible for what activities for the quarter ahead. Remember, this can and should change each quarter to reflect the needs and capacity of each family member.

Remembering the Future
Just imagine your family is flourishing six weeks from now. What are you doing? Talk about it like it's already happened.

The One-Page Plan
Nothing is more useless than a seventeen-page plan that hides in the drawer. At the end of your Family Basecamp, take a moment to summarize the key points for your next twelve-week year on one page:

- The two or three most important priorities for each family member
- The type of support each family member needs
- Important dates
- Key activities that require scheduling (appointments, sports, tutoring, etc.)
- Key things to prepare for the year ahead
- Critical conversations

The outputs from your Family Basecamp will become an integral part of your Weekly Reset.

A gameplan that no one reviews is useless. The hard work and insights from your Family Basecamp need to be accessible and easy to use throughout the year. To ensure this is the case, I recommend you take one of two approaches:

1. Keep it simple: Buy yourself a big-ass calendar. And I mean *big*. Go to your local stationery store and find a calendar that is at least two feet tall. This big-ass calendar is a great way to install a physical presence in your home as a visual reminder of your gameplan. It should also be big enough to hold the goals and commitments of your entire family.

2. Go digital: The best way to keep everyone on the same page is to upload the one-page summary to a digital file that everyone can access. Our favorite tool for this is Maple, a mobile app designed to help you manage your family's busy schedule, allowing you to organize household chores, meal prep, kids' activities, and more, and it's the ideal place to keep your Family Basecamp summary.

When

More than anything, it is important to be consistent in creating space every twelve weeks to meet for Family Basecamp. After supporting many teams and families through this process, I recommend scheduling your Family Basecamps at the following times:

- **August:** Build your gameplan for a great back-to-school (September—October—November)

- **November:** Design a remarkable holiday season, followed by an intentional start to the New Year (December—January—February)

- **February:** Construct your approach for the spring (March—April—May)

- **May:** Design an incredible summer (June—July—August)

Note: This schedule is recommended for a family that is in a stable state. If your family is going through significant change or challenge, I recommend you have a Family Basecamp at least once a month.

The Metronome Effect

Your Family Basecamp sets your focus and direction season by season. But your Weekly Resets act as a metronome to keep everyone moving in the right direction and on the same page.

Okay, I get it. The concept of having a weekly family meeting isn't new and exciting. But are you consistently doing it right now?

The natural question most leaders ask is, How do I spend the time? What are the specific questions we talk about? Do you have an agenda I can follow? While I can help you in all of those areas, I want to stress the importance of focusing on building a consistent and predictable cadence with your weekly resets. The trust that comes from this is huge. If it's a weekly gathering, *do it* weekly. If it's bi-weekly, *do it* bi-weekly. There is no silver-bullet agenda to follow. What is way more important is that your family comes together consistently.

Much like a rocket ship lifting off Planet Earth, the beginning is where you will spend the most energy: enrolling your family members, finding a date, going through the awkwardness of doing anything new for the first time. But once you've reached orbit and gotten a few under your belt, your Weekly Resets will carry a momentum of their own, something you can't live without. You may be reading this wondering, "How the fuck am I going to convince my fourteen-year-old son to ditch his video games or friends to participate in a family meeting?" What a great and honest challenge. When it comes down to deciding how/where/when, it's important to think about how you might make the very act of coming together naturally rewarding in and of itself. Connect over brunch on a Sunday morning. Sit out on the back deck with some ice cream. Bike to a great lookout and pick up your kid's favorite snacks on the way.

Once you have a predictable gathering where you can connect and reset, I've noticed it has a profound impact on the overall tension and anxiety experienced in a family. When you know there will be an opportunity to ask for help, talk about something that bothered you, or share something important to you, you can rest easy more often in the moment.

It also allows you to come to important conversations in the right mindset and readiness. To work on the plumbing when it isn't raining. One of my favorite examples of a leader who embraces the concept of a Family Basecamp is Laura Gassner Otting, author of *Limitless* and *Wonderhell*. We met in 2019 at EPIC, an annual gathering of entrepreneurs, philanthropists, innovators, and collaborators from around the world who come together to learn from and connect with one another.

After day three, Laura and I got to chatting at one of the roundtables as the rest of the guests were making their way back to their rooms before dinner. The essence of our conversation was captured beautifully in one of her blog posts, "The One Meeting Your Need to Add to Your Calendar."

"Let's face it," Laura said, "your company can't crush its goals without your department and team meeting regularly to make sure everyone is staying on track, goals are being met, and morale is high. So, if your company can't crush its goals without them, why would you expect the same results of the members of your household, at least a few of whom probably don't have fully formed frontal lobes yet, without the same tools?"

Now, there isn't a perfect way of hosting a Weekly Reset with your family. Like I said, consistency and predictability are way more important than how you structure it specifically. But here is an outline for your next Weekly Reset.

1 Review the Game Film

In 2022, I had the privilege of going behind the scenes with the Edmonton Oilers, one of Canada's most iconic professional hockey teams. After every game, the coaching staff, equipment managers, and players all come together to watch the game film. Regardless of whether the team won or lost, watching and studying the game film creates the opportunity for everyone to actively reflect on what went well, what broke down, and how they might leverage the experience to get better going forward.

Most families don't have fifty-two great weeks every year, but one week repeated fifty-two times. At the beginning of every Weekly Reset, start by asking your family members to share the highlights from the week before. Take a few moments to talk about why these things were so important and how they happened. This is a great opportunity as a leader to capture your family members doing things well. Most families believe they are too busy to slow down and smell the roses. But by taking a few moments to celebrate, you will keep everyone focused on what it means to win as a family and the great progress you're making week by week. Because let's not forget that happiness is the by-product of making meaningful progress toward a significant goal. As you review the highlights from the week before, take the opportunity to express your gratitude for the role everyone played to make it happen—big or small.

Now, you might be wondering, is this the time to talk about what didn't go well last week? Not yet. We'll get there, but now isn't the time.

2 Plan the Week Ahead

In a study published by the Australian government's Institute of Family Studies, the longest-married couples were pragmatic, didn't expect a perfect marriage, and focused on enjoying their relationship while accommodating their differences. After celebrating some of your progress and momentum, it's time to look at the week ahead to strategize how you will get everything done together as a team.

This is where you go through the week day by day to review who has to be where, at what time, and how it's all going to happen. It's when you discuss what important moments are coming up throughout the week, who needs extra help, and even the basics like what's on the menu for dinner.

The purpose of this is to identify any potential logistical conflicts to make sure what's most important stays most important and that everyone has the support they need to get done what's most important to them. This should be an extremely collaborative time together, leaving everyone feeling clear and supported for the week ahead.

The reality is, your family may not be priority number one each and every week. And that's okay. If you're living your life to the fullest, there will be weeks and moments when your family needs to slide down on the priority scale. What isn't okay is assuming they understand the importance and magnitude of your priorities. The whole intention of this part of the Weekly Reset is to get on the same page, proactively identify any issues, and get clear on how everyone can support each other to be successful.

3 Look Around the Corner

While the primary focus for these family meetings should be on winning this week, it is always helpful to paddle before the wave. Or, as I often say, "look around corners."

After dialing in your week ahead, this is where you pull out your Family Basecamp summary to check in on your twelve-week plan. Take a moment to review any upcoming travel, vacations, sport tournaments, movies you want to see, big school events, birthday parties, and other significant commitments. This will allow everyone to maintain awareness of what's coming and mitigate the risk of you forgetting important details.

And as you know from experience, plan A often becomes plan F. This is also a great opportunity to communicate and share any changes of plans or new information your family needs to adapt around.

By reconnecting with what's coming up over the next few weeks, you can proactively identify anything that needs to be done this week to make next week great.

4 Airing of Grievances

Ahhh, now the fun stuff. As you near the end of your meeting, you will have positive energy building in your family and a bunch of clarity about what's going on this week and coming down the pipe.

This is when you want to take a few moments to air grievances and talk about what *didn't* go well the week before. One of the things I learned from Laura Gassner Otting was the importance of striking while the iron is cold.

One of Laura's blog posts beautifully illustrates how stupid and futile it can be at times to try to correct someone's behavior when you are emotional and angry. "Never in the history of my family has anyone said, 'Hey, I love that you are yelling at me, and I am able to really step back and think about what you are trying to say through your frustration and anger, and I feel in no way emotionally attached to the corner into which I've backed myself... so, yeah, you're right, I'll change my behavior right away. Please accept my deeply felt apologies for my obvious transgressions.'"

Whether you're leading at home or at work, it is important that you connect before you correct. When you share issues and challenges in a non-emotional state, the likelihood of your family members understanding the situation and the impact it had on others is significantly higher. The aim of the airing of grievances is to do exactly that: air them. If you need more time to talk about someone's intention or adjust your interpretation of their actions, it's best to find a separate time to do that.

The greatest opportunity here, however, is to use this as a time to demonstrate to your children what it looks like to repair conflict in a healthy way. Most kids only get to see their parents fight; the issue is usually resolved privately after the kids go to bed or leave for a friend's house. By airing grievances in your Weekly Reset, you are creating regular opportunities to repair and reconnect. As the Chief Family Officer, it is important you come prepared to take ownership of your shortcomings and lead by example. And don't forget to reward and recognize your family members for doing the same when their time comes.

5 Schedule the Next Weekly Reset

As you wrap up your meeting together, it's super important that everyone take out their calendars and confirm the date, time, and location of your next Weekly Reset. Chris Ronzio, CEO of Trainual, calls these meetings Wine Wednesdays, where he and his wife meet over a delicious glass of wine to plan the week ahead and regroup before a busy weekend with the kids. As his kids got older and the weekdays became busier, they started meeting on Sunday nights over a decaf coffee, and now call their regroup Decaf Discussions. But when you host your Weekly Reset is entirely up to you. Like I said earlier, what is most important is that these quick and simple connections remain predictable and consistent. It's as simple as that.

So, when will you hold your first Family Basecamp?

Next Play

Systems of living are the backbone of your family operating system. Let's start working on yours.

1 How does your family stay on the same page now?

1. How does your family come together to plan and strategize currently?
2. When was the last time you had a family meeting?
3. What happens when your family doesn't regroup regularly?
4. Take a few moments to schedule your Family Basecamp and Weekly Resets for the next three months.

For the Family Basecamp, specify a date and time; for the Weekly Resets, specify the day of the week and time (e.g., Sunday morning over breakfast or Wednesday night after the kids go to bed).

2 Host your first Family Basecamp!

On your next date night or family dinner, share the concept of the Family Basecamp with those you love. Ask them how it would make a positive impact on your family, and work together to design and schedule your first Family Basecamp experience.

9

Beginning Again

SEVERAL YEARS after writing to my dad to tell him I never wanted to be like him, I wrote to him again. This time, instead of telling him to fuck off, I crafted my one last letter: a letter filled with the things I would want to say if this were the final opportunity to speak my heart and mind to the man who had brought me into this world. Unlike my first letter, which was filled with accusations, comparison, judgment, and anger, this one was filled with forgiveness, admiration, respect, and appreciation for everything my dad has done for me over the years, knowingly or otherwise.

Although we had reconnected since I had returned from Hawaii, I began to ask myself if I was happy with our relationship. It was clear to me that while I was happy with where we were at, I did want to deepen our relationship and spend more time together. I wanted to get to know my dad better and start to understand his journey through life. I wanted to carve out more space to experience effortless belonging and find ourselves laughing again. And even if our relationship never returned to the quintessential father-son dynamic, I knew damn well that in my version of winning, I wanted him to become one of my friends.

I remember the feeling in my stomach as I approached the same mailbox I had punched almost a decade earlier. Like last time, tears were streaming down my face. The only difference was that this go-round, a subtle smile formed on my face as I ran my hands over the small dent wedged on the right side. After I slowly placed the envelope in the chute, I closed my eyes and took a big deep breath.

So much had happened in my life between these letters. Unbeknownst to me at the time, the pain I had gone through earlier was responsible for creating the perspective and gifts I have today. I realized as I let go of that letter that for many years the anger and frustration I had held for my dad acted as a glass ceiling to my personal growth and success. At that moment, that glass ceiling was now the floor I stood on.

A few days later, while I was out for a walk, my phone rang. I looked down and saw my dad calling. I knew he had received my letter and was calling to talk. While we didn't know what this would look like, we made a choice to begin again. And since then, we've rebuilt a wonderful relationship and continue to deepen our friendship to this day. Over time I've become inspired by my dad's view of the world, his generosity and care for others, the way he makes decisions, and the amount of respect he has for the opinions and ideas of others. Especially those he disagrees with. And I've also learned that some of my most painful memories were based on a story half told. By sharing my pain with my dad and being curious, I've been able to better understand the many variables that influenced the relationship I had with him growing up and that my over-simplified story that "my dad's a workaholic and doesn't care about me" wasn't true.

While I am grateful, it's difficult to not feel like we've wasted a significant amount of our lives together. But as my beloved mentor Philip McKernan always says, "Your greatest gifts are found beside your greatest pains." Without this hardship in my life, I wouldn't have turned into the person I am today or become such a devoted dad. Rather than experiencing this as regret, I use the pain from this experience to remind me why it is so important to lead my family and invest the energy to understand the stories they tell themselves about our relationship together. Especially when it's hard. I hope I can inspire you and my children to do the same.

And as I did with my father, you always have an opportunity to take ownership and begin again.

The Right Next Thing

In game theory there are two distinctly different types of games: infinite and finite.

A finite game is played for the purpose of winning. For a game to be finite, there must be clear rules, agreed-upon boundaries, and a clear winner and loser as a result. In a finite game, players seek to accumulate power over time and evaluate their worth based on what they have accumulated.

An infinite game, however, is an entirely different animal. Unlike a finite game, the goal of an infinite game is simply continuing to play the game itself. There is no finish line and no declared winner or loser along the way. There are no clearly defined rules, and if there are rules, they can change at any time. The players are known and unknown. The game is done when a person drops out because they have lost the resources and energy to continue playing.

Building and leading your family is an infinite game through and through. While it's great to play to win, you can change the definition of what it means to win at any time. As your family grows and matures through various seasons of life, you will be surprised. As James Carse says in *Finite and Infinite Games*, "To be prepared against surprise is to be trained. To be prepared for surprise is to be educated."

If you play the game of life as an infinite game, instead of focusing on how things *should be*, you can instead focus on leading your family to adapt to the unknowns.

At the end of the day, this is what it means to be a Chief Family Officer. It isn't about having a vision and gameplan to build the perfect family. Instead, it's all about making the most of the cards you're dealt and embracing the artistry of lifestyle design. It's about adapting your approach and choosing to change your rules so you can stay in the game as long as possible. Remember, every day is day one.

Throughout this book, I introduced you to three important landscapes of family leadership:

1. Family strategy
2. Systems of living
3. Relational excellence

These three landscapes make up the foundation of your family. Each feeding the others will make the foundation for your family to stand upon. Over time, you will experience strength in each of these areas. And at times, you will experience weakness and need to revisit the fundamentals to get back on track.

It is my hope that after reading this book, you've been inspired to step into your role as Chief Family Officer. But where do you start?

Regardless of where you start, it's important to accept that you can't do everything at once. Success and momentum come from doing the right next thing after the right next thing after the right next thing. So here are a few first steps that will help you prepare to embark on your journey.

Get Your Partner on Board

Unlike with most personal development books, your success implementing what you've learned here is highly dependent on your spouse or partner being on board. While they certainly don't need to lead the charge, it is important that you both get on the same page and see the value in putting in the work together to build your family by design.

Instead of coming home with a bunch of enthusiasm and ideas to get started, remember that *people do things for their reasons, not yours*. It would be very easy to start by sharing the things you want to start doing right away and all the things you've learned. While this is important, it's not the best place to start. Instead, approach your partner with an understanding of why they might see value and benefit in doing this work together. The answer is found by asking yourself this question: "What would my partner's number one complaint be about me and our family?"

Depending on how well you know your partner, there is a good chance your answer won't be perfect. In fact, you might be *way* off. And that's perfect. Once you have a guess, the first thing to do is create an opportunity to talk with your partner to test your assumption.

After helping his daughter choose to step down from provincial soccer for a year, Martin, from Chapter 5, immediately saw the value in this work and wanted to get started with his wife. He is a shining example of how to approach your partner to get on the same page.

After we helped Samantha make her decision, it was clear to me that we had lots of opportunities to improve how we were making decisions and working together as a family. It's hard to not want to do everything right away once you realize there is work to be done. Carolyn and I have a strong relationship, but I knew that if I brought home a "family operating system," there was a good chance that she was going to roll her eyes. I can hear her now: "Oh Martin, the last thing we need here is one of your work tools or strategy playbooks to operate our family." Right or wrongly, I knew that our family would benefit a ton from revisiting what it means to win together as a family now that our kids were getting so much older and nearing university or college. I guessed that Carolyn's number one complaint about me would be that I am not present enough with the kids when we are all together. After dinner one night, I asked Carolyn if I was correct. To my surprise, she had something different in mind. I learned that she was actually quite happy with how present I had been around the house recently. Carolyn instead shared that her biggest complaint right now was that we always worked to carve out extra time for me to go out with my guy friends for golf, but we never carved out space for her to do stuff that she loved, such as painting. I'll be honest, I thought she gave up on painting a long time ago and had no idea that she wanted to get back into it so bad. Bringing this up with Carolyn taught me a lot. And it also opened up a window for me to ask her if she would be open to learning about a few things that would help us buy back more time for both her and I to do more of the things we loved now that the kids were older and more independent.

Remember, the goal here is to work together to build your family by design so that everyone can win—you, your partner, and your family. Everyone will have their own reasons and goals for investing the time and energy into this work. It's your job to figure that out. Start there, and get your partner on board.

Pick One Thing

One of the main reasons so many people fail to follow through on their goals is that they set way too many of them. I can't tell you how many leaders I've met who have a list of seventeen goals they want to accomplish and live in a constant state of feeling behind on everything. No shit. They could make progress on half of them but still go to bed each and every night thinking about what they didn't do or how far behind they are. This negative self-talk doesn't help anyone build confidence and momentum.

Instead, I would much rather see you choose one thing you want to improve and *nail it*. Pick one thing, make progress, see the results, and move on to something else after you've integrated the work.

Remember Meredith back in Chapter 7, who hadn't spent one-on-one time with her husband Steven for the last two years? After juggling an overwhelming amount of work commitments and an ever-busy sport and extracurricular calendar for her kids, her right next step is to focus on buying back time so she and Steven have more capacity to connect with one another without compromising their commitments to work and quality time with their children.

During one of the kids' soccer practices, Steven and Meredith left their phones in the truck and used the time to explore a few approaches, and they decided to hire their old babysitter one night a week to tidy up the house after dinner, play with the kids, and put them to bed. This help gave them the space to enjoy a glass of wine together after dinner without having to clean up, to go out for dinner themselves, to play together as a family or, depending on the week, to do a bit more work before heading to bed. If this sounds like you, your systems of living would be the place to start.

Or let's reflect on Claire from Chapter 4, who redefined what it meant to win as a family. For Claire, so much had changed over the last few years, yet she hadn't taken the time yet to regroup and reset. By carving out time to talk about what it means to win together as a family, Claire and her husband were able to anchor in the present moment and get on the same page. The clarity from this discussion empowered them to make the conscious decision to separate. A difficult decision, but the right one. If you've gone through significant change recently, family strategy is likely a great place to begin.

Or perhaps Alissa and Mark from Chapter 6 best illustrate your current reality. On the outside, they had it all, but behind the scenes the stress of being in conflict day to day was getting in the way of them pursuing their dreams. For Alissa and Mark, making the choice to learn how to repair conflict effectively and establishing agreements for future conflicts brought them back on the same team. By focusing on this first, they were able to learn about one another, dissolve a big pile of resentment, and start proactively creating the space to invest in their most important relationship. Improving how they repaired conflict equipped them with the capacity to start working on other aspects of their family without a blowout. If day-to-day conflict and tension get in the way of you working together as a team, relational excellence is your first step.

Regardless of where you are today, it is your job as Chief Family Officer to discover your right next step. To do that, all you need to do is answer one question: "What is the one thing we can do that would make everything else easier?"

Take a Professional Approach

At the highest level, winning is a team sport. As with any good group workout, the accountability and inspiration that come from working alongside others can help us find our personal edge and dig deep. And as with any new skill, most people learn more effectively by witnessing others in action.

As you step into this journey of becoming a Chief Family Officer, it's important that you build a support system around you and your family. When it comes to building an ecosystem of support, a few different approaches work well.

1 Hire a coach! It's difficult to be a coach and player at the same time. Winning is highly dependent on being able to remain attuned to the emerging unmet needs of your family, challenging yourself to build your own relational skills, and deciding what the right next thing is for your family to focus on. Doing all of that while working hard and enjoying quality time with your family is a tall order.

When you make a decision to hire a coach, you are significantly increasing your odds of success for two main reasons. First, you are collapsing time. Coaches will help you learn from their mistakes and successes and allow you to bring your best energy and focus to the work. More importantly, adding a coach to the mix will help make sure you and your spouse have a shared understanding of the problems you are solving. Doing any personal development is difficult at the best of times. By adding your partner to the mix, you are now managing and developing a system, not just a person. A professional coach will help you find your way.

2 Find mentors. Professional coaching is highly effective, but another support model that works really well is to establish a mentor/mentee relationship with another couple you look up to. This should be a couple in your life who knows you well but is far enough along in their relationship that they have experienced and overcome many of the challenges in front of you. Most importantly, they should have a relationship that inspires you. In my experience, leaders who have actively worked on their family and relationships are highly motivated to help others in their journey.

This type of relationship and support can be as formal or informal as you need it. Whether it's grabbing dinner together every couple of months or setting up a regular touch point together, establishing a mentor/mentee relationship will keep you honest and create an outlet to work on challenges and celebrate the good stuff along the way.

3 Build community. Lastly, another great option is to build your own community and circle of friends to do this work alongside one another. There is a good chance your family is surrounded by other like-minded families who share similar interests and values. Today, so many of us try to solve problems on our own that traditionally have been supported by the community. And yet, we wonder why we are struggling so much at times. If the call to lead your family has inspired you, there is a good chance your community will be inspired as well.

Good friends of ours, Michael and Adee, are a great example of this. Living in Dripping Springs, Texas, Michael and Adee have a small group of ten friends (five couples) all with young children near a similar age. While personal growth and development has always been a thread that connected everyone, a few years ago they collectively acknowledged the power of community and agreed to actively support one another in their journeys. Every month their community meets together as a whole, followed by a men's and women's gathering to create space for intimate conversations to support and challenge each other. At the core of their community is an explicit commitment to look out for each other's family and relationship at large. That means there is no room for bitching behind your partner's back or taking sides. Instead, each person agrees to stand up and look out for their relationship as a whole. When you take a community approach like this, not only can you learn from others, but you also create an environment in which you can begin to teach and share from your own experiences. Throughout my life, teaching others has been a big part of my learning process, cementing my understanding of principles and concepts.

Family Operating System Upgrade

Every few months, a little notification pops up in the top-right corner of my MacBook Pro: "Software Update Available." And it gives me two simple options: "Install." And "Not Now."

When it comes to updating computer software, only about 54 percent of users typically install the updates. And even of those who do, roughly 65 percent delay the updates and opt for the "Remind Me Later" option. Most people don't do software upgrades because they are unconvinced that the new features will be useful. They're scared to embrace the danger of difference. As with any change, what is familiar (even if it's not great) is always perceived to be safer than the unknown. Inevitably, most begrudgingly wait until the moment of truth, when not upgrading puts your success or ability to work in jeopardy. And of course, this always seems to happen right before a big meeting or project deadline. Exactly the worst time.

You see, change comes from choice. And choice comes from conflict. As you near the end of this book, I am prompting you with the opportunity to upgrade your family operating system and embrace the next evolution of your leadership at home. No one can force you to change. It is up to you to choose whether you want to click "Install Now" or "Remind Me Later."

Throughout your life, you will find yourself crossing new thresholds. Moments in your life when you enter a new beginning and mark the ending of a previous chapter or era. Some are thresholds you will choose to cross. And many are ones you will never be able to anticipate. Regardless of the motivation, successfully crossing a threshold demands courage and trust—trust that the best is yet to come.

So, at which threshold are you standing now in your life? What new chapter do you have the opportunity to enter?

There's one more thing. The choice to upgrade your personal operating system is not as simple as hitting "Install Now" and leaving your machine to load while you grab a snack and call your mom. If you and your partner are ready to cross this threshold together, the best way to take this step is by actively creating a moment of significance. A ceremony.

Throughout time, ceremony has been used to formally represent a decision—a line that demarcates what was from what will be. The moment where you decide to sunset your old way of being and start the journey of discovering and learning how to fully embrace your new way. Throughout your life, you have experienced, participated in, or perhaps even hosted ceremonies yourself. Weddings, birthdays, funerals, retirement parties, baptisms, bat mitzvahs, or tapping the keg at Oktoberfest. There is a never-ending list of variations to ceremony, but regardless of how it comes together, the common denominator of all ceremony is the act of witnessing an *intention*.

If you and your partner are ready to cross this threshold together, I encourage you to host a ceremony to create a moment that captures this inflection point and evolution in your story. A moment to express your commitment to one another and pay respect to all the experiences that have brought you to where you are today.

Now, ceremony is a sacred experience. If your knee-jerk reaction is to book a venue, invite all your family and friends, hire a DJ, and make a night of it... you're missing the point. While there is a time and place for elaborate and expensive celebrations, this is not one of them. Instead, this ceremony should be between you and your partner. A private moment filled with reverence and intention for who you want to become, both as a family and as individuals.

Here are a few simple steps to crafting a ceremony to celebrate your choice.

1 Pick a Time and Space

Without time and space, ceremony won't happen. And this isn't something you wing at the last minute. Take a few moments together to select a space where you can insulate yourselves from the outside world and a moment in time when you can come together without distraction or sudden interruption. The space for this ceremony should be in a place of solitude, where you are separated from any outside inputs or stimuli. Take a few minutes together to discuss what things could potentially distract or demand your attention. Work through each of these to proactively manage them so it doesn't happen.

While there are a variety of types of ceremonies, I strongly encourage you to create a fire for your ceremony. Throughout history, fire ceremonies have been held for healing, for rites of passage, and to mark critical moments when we let go of our past and start new beginnings. Fire is powerful and cleansing, and it connects us to the essential elements of life. This is an important variable in your ceremony and will help determine the space you choose to come together.

2 Set Your Intention

You don't want to show up to the space you've created and think about your intentions on the spot. Leading up to your time together, talk about your intentions and why you are doing this to get on the same page. Ask questions such as these:

- What threshold are we standing at together right now?
- What new standard do we want to hold ourselves to?
- What are we grieving and letting go of?
- What is required of each of us to create the change we seek?
- How can we best support each other on the other side?

3 The Preparation Container

Your ceremony begins in the days leading up to the time and space you've created. It is important to purify your body and mind for the experience ahead of time. In many ceremonial cultures, participants are asked to abstain from any alcohol or recreational drugs for four days leading up to the ceremony. When it comes to preparing for your ceremony, I would ask that you do the same. Alcohol and recreational drugs are a great way to habitually dissociate from our negative emotions. Not only will sobriety allow you to bring your full presence to the ceremony, but it will also create the conditions for you to become more attuned to your emotional experience leading up to the ceremony itself. Pay attention to how you feel and think in the moments and days before your ceremony. This is all a part of your personal process of letting go.

Prior to the ceremony, you will also want to assemble an offering for the fire. An offering is an expression of gratitude and acknowledgment of the universal forces that have brought you to this moment and support you through the process of change. Offerings come in a variety of forms. Fundamentally, the offering should be a sincere gathering of something that can be put into the fire, such as food, herbs, or objects of significance. The idea is that you are giving a sacrifice. For example, instead of enjoying food yourself, you are offering it to the fire in exchange for being supported. By building this, you are engaging your whole being in the process of transformation and going beyond the intellectual exercise of verbalizing or thinking that you want to make a change. The one thing you do not want to include in your offering, however, is photographs of people.

4 The Ceremony

After lighting your fire, take a few moments to stand in silence together to become present to the moment and be where your feet are. With your offerings in hand, share your intentions out loud with each other. This is a perfect time to express the answers to the questions you explored in the days leading up to this ceremony. Share what behaviors, actions, or pain you would like to leave behind, and state the intentions, aspirations, and desires you have together for the future. Part of this process is acknowledging that there are universal forces much bigger than ourselves, and in this moment we are asking for their support and help.

Once this is done, both of you should place your offerings in the fire while taking a moment to acknowledge the importance of what just took place. Take some time to enjoy each other's company by the fire, immersing yourself in the experience together. Notice how each of you feels in the moments immediately following your ceremony.

Over the coming days, pay attention to how this ceremony has shifted the dynamic and experience of your presence together. It's important to expect that in the days following the ceremony, many of the behaviors or patterns you parted ways with will likely show up again. Please know that this is not a sign of failure but a very normal part of the healing and transformation process.

At the end of the day, this is your ceremony. Make it yours and feel free to add any details of significance. By following these guidelines and adding details to make it your own, you are sure to create an experience that you will forever remember as a milestone in your journey together.

Ceremony is not a magic trick. Reinvention takes place through the small actions you take every day. You can make a decision to change, but there is still all the work that comes. Expect that it will be difficult at the beginning, messy in the middle, and beautiful at the end. The process will take time and challenge you along the way. Hearing about the challenges other families go through helps everyone feel less incapable of doing it themselves. Share your story with others. Listen to theirs. And never forget that the work will work on you more than you will work on it.

Leading your family and becoming a Chief Family Officer can be the single greatest adventure of your life—an adventure that with grace, intellectual humility, self-awareness, and love will shape you into the person you want to become. The type of person who is a transitional character in your family story and a beacon of possibility who inspires and creates the conditions for those around you to thrive.

If ever you're lost and unsure of what to do next, just ask yourself, What would love do now?

Acknowledgments

THIS BOOK is a result of the collective experiences I've had throughout my life, but there are a few select individuals who have been champions and catalysts for the personal development that has helped me become the author, leader, and parent I am today.

Philip McKernan, an enlightened hooligan, my coach, and the man who said what no one else had the courage to. Thank you for holding me to a higher standard than I had for myself and helping me embrace forgiveness and own my gifts and talents. Without you, I'd still be working some corporate consulting gig and marinating in resentment and anger.

Ranj Bawa, my lighthouse and big brother. Whenever I was struggling, lost, and unsure of where to go next, you always picked up the phone and guided my journey with purpose and love. Whether it was helping me and Jen navigate the unexpected journey of welcoming

William into this world or crafting my approach as a professional coach, you have been both the shoulder I've cried on and the place I've come to celebrate. You will forever be family to me.

Dr. James Rouse, you are the man who inspired me to disrupt mediocrity and change my life. Your presence and zest for life awakened a tiger inside me that was dormant for many years. You will never truly understand the impression you've made on me. Your blessings and love are deeply woven into my leadership at home and at work.

Michael Cazayoux, my dear friend. Thank you for walking alongside me through some of the most significant conversations and moments in my life. You have shown me what true vulnerability looks like and what it means to be a great friend. I can't wait to see where life brings us to together.

Phil Jones, the man who saw the potential in this book. Without you, I would have never met Trena White and the team from Page Two and embarked on the journey to become an author. You are a beacon of possibility in my life, and in so many ways an example of who I am striving to become. Your tenacity for life and care for others inspires me deeply.

Steve Farlow, the man who supported me to find my footing and begin my journey as an entrepreneur. Not only did you create the conditions for me to embrace this path in life, but you also were an example of the dad and man that I wanted to become. You planted a seed in me years ago that is just starting to sprout. I am forever grateful for our friendship.

Dr. Greg Wells, renowned health and high-performance expert. Your journey to excellence after breaking your back set the bar for me. Without you, I would have never embarked on my Ironman journey and reclaimed my health. Every man stands on the shoulders of giants. You are a giant in my life.

Jayson Gaddis, my mentor, coach, and teacher. Your work saved my family and is the reason why Jen and I have the thriving relationship we do today. Thank you for challenging me to become more vulnerable and develop the relational skills I needed to rise to challenges we faced at home. I am forever grateful for the mentorship and learning you've offered me over the years. You are the reason I made the choice to become a couples coach and start working with families. Without you, I would never have seen this as a possibility. And to be honest, I'd probably be divorced by now if it wasn't for your leadership.

Tonia and Andy Blenkarn, my dear friends and clients. At a critical moment in my journey to publish this book, you were there and answered my call. Your generosity and love were instrumental in creating a space for me to close a significant chapter of healing in my life... *and* write the final chapter of this book. I will forever remember the time I spent in your beautiful family cottage. It truly is one of the "thinnest" places in the world.

My dad, Gord. I wouldn't change a thing about the way our relationship has unfolded. I am so proud to call you my dad and grateful that we still have so much life left to enjoy with one another. Thank you for all the ways you've supported me over the years, especially those that have gone unseen or not acknowledged. Your friendship and presence in my life matters more than you know.

Daniel Leonard, my teacher and the man who has been behind the scenes. No one knows me like you do. Thank you for helping me navigate the dark and find the light in my life. The wisdom and teachings you've gifted me over the years are imbued throughout these pages. You've helped me navigate and make peace with the unseen elements of life. You know how much I love you.

My mom, Sue. Thank you for always being there for me. Thank you for loving me in my most difficult moments, even when you were the one who had to bear the brunt of my frustrations growing up. I promise I won't jersey you again. While I didn't share any of our experiences together in this book, you must know that your guidance, love, and friendship are why I am able to write such a book in the first place. You've taught me what unconditional love is and feels like. If I can love Quinn, Kalem, and William a fraction of how much you've loved me, I will be proud of the parent I've become. You will forever me my mommabear.

Notes

1: Leading Your Most Important Team

6   *"There are many experiences in life…":* Jen Forristal, *The Umbrella Effect: Your Guide to Raising Strong, Adaptable Kids in a Stressful World* (Austin, TX: Lioncrest, 2022), 26.

7   *And according to the United States National Center:* CDC/NCHS National Vital Statistics System, "Provisional Number of Marriages and Marriage Rate: United States, 2000–2019" and "Provisional Number of Divorces and Annulments and Rate: United States, 2000–2019," n.d., cdc.gov/nchs/data/dvs/national-marriage-divorce-rates-00-19.pdf.

12   *Gino Wickman, author of* Traction: Gino Wickman, *Traction: Get a Grip on Your Business* (Dallas, TX: BenBella Books, 2012), xi–xii.

12   *As Roger Martin, author of* Playing to Win: A.G. Lafley and Roger L. Martin, *Playing to Win: How Strategy Really Works* (Boston: Harvard Business Review Press, 2013), 35.

14   *When the stakes are high:* Jayson Gaddis, *Getting to Zero: How to Work through Conflict in Your High-Stakes Relationships* (New York: Hachette Go, 2022), 86.

17   *During a recent couples experience:* Jayson Gaddis, live session delivered at Confluence Event, Stratford, ON, November 2022.

17   *Once you've done this:* Gaddis, *Getting to Zero*, 147.
18   *According to Stats Canada:* Sharanjit Uppal, "Employment Patterns of Families with Children," Statistics Canada, 2015, www150.statcan.gc.ca/n1/pub/75-006-x/2015001/article/14202-eng.htm.
18   *Yet while much has changed:* Eve Rodsky, *Fair Play: A Game-Changing Solution for When You Have Too Much to Do (and More Life to Live)* (New York: G.P. Putnam's Sons, 2019), 7.

2: Your Family Will Change You

29   *As podcaster Chris Williamson said:* Chris Williamson, "Chris Williamson: The Shocking New Research on Why Men and Women Are No Longer Compatible!" *Diary of a CEO*, episode 237, April 10, 2023, video, 2:07:19, youtube.com/watch?v=K2tGt2XWd9Q.
34   *As Brené Brown eloquently points out:* Brené Brown, *Daring Greatly: How the Courage to Be Vulnerable Transforms the Way We Live, Love, Parent, and Lead* (New York: Avery, 2015), 145.
34   *One of my personal mentors, Jayson Gaddis:* Jayson Gaddis, *Getting to Zero: How to Work through Conflict in Your High-Stakes Relationships* (New York: Hachette Go, 2022), 86.
37   *In* Immunity to Change: Robert Kegan and Lisa Laskow Lahey, *Immunity to Change: How to Overcome It and Unlock the Potential in Yourself and Your Organization* (Boston: Harvard Business Review Press, 2009), 17.
39   *As Todd eloquently explains in his book:* Todd Herman, *The Alter Ego Effect: The Power of Secret Identities to Transform Your Life* (New York: Harper Business, 2019), 3–4.
39   *A team of researchers out of the University of Minnesota:* Rachel E. White, Emily O. Prager, Catherine Schaefer, Ethan Kross, Angela L. Duckworth, and Stephanie M. Carlson, "The 'Batman Effect': Improving Perseverance in Young Children," *Child Development* 88, no. 5 (September/October 2017): 1563–71, doi.org/10.1111/cdev.12695.

3: It's Not What You Look at That Matters, It's What You See

48 *Predictive disgust from a place of superiority:* Ellie Lisitsa, "The Four Horsemen: Criticism, Contempt, Defensiveness, and Stone-Walling," Gottman Institute, n.d., gottman.com/blog/the-four-horsemen-recognizing-criticism-contempt-defensiveness-and-stonewalling.

48 *World-renowned relationship expert:* John Gottman, *Why Marriages Succeed or Fail: And How You Can Make Yours Last* (New York: Simon & Schuster, 1995), 79–80.

49 *The illusion here is something called:* Anina Rich and Sarah Maguire, "What is the Baader-Meinhof Phenomenon?" Lighthouse, Macquarie University, July 22, 2020, lighthouse.mq.edu.au/article/july-2020/What-is-the-Baader-Meinhof-Phenomenon.

50 *Stephen Covey illustrates this beautifully:* Stephen R. Covey, *The 7 Habits of Highly Effective Families: Creating a Nurturing Family in a Turbulent World* (New York: St. Martin's Essentials, 2022), 17.

51 *If you've never heard of them before:* Liesl Barrell, "Everything You Always Wanted to Know About B-Corporations (but Were Afraid to Ask)," Third Wunder (blog), January 19, 2015, thirdwunder.com/blog/what-are-b-corporations.

52 *Today, dozens of international mining companies:* Joe Rogan and Siddharth Kara, "The Disturbing Reality of Cobalt Mining for Rechargeable Batteries," *PowerfulJRE*, December 22, 2022, video, 14:44, youtube.com/watch?v=CIWvk3gJ_7E; Todd C. Frankel, "The Cobalt Pipeline," *Washington Post*, September 30, 2016, washingtonpost.com/graphics/business/batteries/congo-cobalt-mining-for-lithium-ion-battery; Nicolas Niarchos, "The Dark Side of Congo's Cobalt Rush," *New Yorker*, May 24, 2021, newyorker.com/magazine/2021/05/31/the-dark-side-of-congos-cobalt-rush.

54 *The triple bottom line is a management framework:* Barrell, "Everything You Always Wanted to Know About B-Corporations."

59   *We know that social isolation:* National Center for Chronic Disease Prevention and Health Promotion, "Loneliness and Social Isolation Linked to Serious Health Conditions," Centers for Disease Control and Prevention, April 29, 2021, cdc.gov/aging/publications/features/lonely-older-adults.html.

4: Playing to Win

73   *When it comes to building a winning strategy:* Roger L. Martin, "The Big Lie of Strategic Planning," *Harvard Business Review*, January-February 2014, hbr.org/2014/01/the-big-lie-of-strategic-planning.

74   *"What I have observed over and over...":* Stephen R. Covey, *The 7 Habits of Highly Effective Families: Creating a Nurturing Family in a Turbulent World* (New York: St. Martin's Essentials, 2022), 98–99.

77   *According to the World Health Organization:* World Health Organization, "The World Health Report 2001: Mental Disorders Affect One in Four People," September 28, 2001, who.int/news/item/28-09-2001-the-world-health-report-2001-mental-disorders-affect-one-in-four-people.

77   *In Canada, where my family lives:* Mental Health Commission of Canada, *Making the Case for Investing in Mental Health in Canada*, 2016, mentalhealthcommission.ca/wp-content/uploads/drupal/2016-06/Investing_in_Mental_Health_FINAL_Version_ENG.pdf.

5: Using Pain as a Tool

105 *Phil has taught me that there are:* Phil M. Jones, live session, March 2022, exactlywhattosay.com.

6: Protecting Your Most Important Asset: Relationships

118 *We know from great studies:* George E. Vaillant, *Triumphs of Experience: The Men of the Harvard Grant Study* (Cambridge, MA: Belknap Press, 2012); Michael Miller, "What Makes a Good Life? Three Lessons on Life, Love, and Decision Making from the Harvard Grant Study," Six Seconds, April 19, 2021, 6seconds.org/2021/04/19/harvard-grant-study.

122 *If you've read* The Five Love Languages: Gary Chapman, *The Five Love Languages: How to Express Heartfelt Commitment to Your Mate* (Bhopal, India: Manjul Publishing House, 2009).

124 *In his book* His Needs, Her Needs: Willard F. Harley Jr., *His Needs, Her Needs: Building a Marriage that Lasts* (Grand Rapids, MI: Revell, 2020).

132 *As Oliver Burkeman points out:* Oliver Burkeman, *Four Thousand Weeks: Time Management for Mortals* (New York: Penguin Random House, 2021).

133 *Jim introduced me to a strategy:* Jim Sheils, *The Family Board Meeting: You Have 18 Summers to Create Lasting Connection with Your Children* (18Summers, 2018).

7: Designing Your Lived Experience

150 *Dan Martell taught me this:* Dan Martell, *Buy Back Your Time: Get Unstuck, Reclaim Your Freedom, and Build Your Empire* (New York: Portfolio/Penguin, 2023), 42.

8: Staying Connected and Aligned

164 *"Hurt, disappointment, and frustration…":* Mitch Temple, *The Marriage Turnaround: How Thinking Differently About Your Relationship Can Change Everything* (Chicago: Moody Publishers, 2008), 72.

166 *"It happens all the time…":* Brian P. Moran and Michael Lennington, *The 12 Week Year: Get More Done in 12 Weeks than Others Do in 12 Months* (Hoboken, NJ: Wiley, 2013), 12.

175 *The essence of our conversation:* Laura Gassner Otting, "The One Meeting You Need to Add to Your Calendar," Laura Gassner Otting (blog), June 13, 2018, lauragassnerotting.com/blog/2018/06/13/family-meeting.

176 *In a study published by the Australian government's:* Robyn Parker, "Why Marriages Last: A Discussion of the Literature," Australian Institute of Family Studies, July 2002, aifs.gov.au/sites/default/files/publication-documents/RP28_0.pdf.

178 *"Never in the history of my family…":* Gassner Otting, "The One Meeting You Need to Add to Your Calendar."

9: Beginning Again

186 *As James Carse says:* James P. Carse, *Finite and Infinite Games: A Vision of Life as Play and Possibility* (New York: Free Press, 2013), 17.

195 *When it comes to updating computer software:* Prashanth Rajivan, Efrat Aharonov-Majar, and Cleotilde Gonzalez, "Update Now or Later? Effects of Experience, Cost, and Risk Preference on Update Decisions," *Journal of Cybersecurity* 6, no. 1 (2020), doi.org/10.1093/cybsec/tyaa002.

195 *And choice comes from conflict:* Tamsen Webster, *Find Your Red Thread: Make Your Big Ideas Irresistible* (Vancouver: Page Two, 2021), 93.

PHOTO: TIMOTHY MUZA

About the Author

DAVE INGLIS is a professional couples and leadership coach, speaker, and author who has spent his career helping companies and leaders navigate their most defining moments. With a unique ability to work at the intersection of business and personal development, Dave shows others how to turn foundational business systems and strategies into deeply transformational personal practices. Outside of business, Dave is a shamanic practitioner and the founder of Strategic Solitude, where he creates experiences for leaders to have the space to pause, be alone, and begin again. Dave lives in Waterloo, Canada, with his wife, Dr. Jen Forristal, and their three children.

Connect with Dave!

Want to work with Dave or ask him to speak at your next event?

Go to **daveinglis.ca** to get in touch with Dave's team, place bulk book orders, and learn more about working with Dave directly.

www.ingramcontent.com/pod-product-compliance
Lightning Source LLC
Chambersburg PA
CBHW060559080526
44585CB00013B/618